How to Use a
Meat Cleaver

HOW TO USE A
MEAT CLEAVER

Secrets and Recipes
from a Mob Family's Kitchen

RENEE, JENNIFER, AND LANA GRAZIANO

A PERIGEE BOOK

A PERIGEE BOOK
Published by the Penguin Group
Penguin Group (USA) LLC
375 Hudson Street, New York, New York 10014

USA • Canada • UK • Ireland • Australia • New Zealand • India • South Africa • China

penguin.com

A Penguin Random House Company

Library of Congress Cataloging-in-Publication Data

Graziano, Renee.
How to use a meat cleaver : secrets and recipes from a mob family's kitchen / Renee, Jennifer, and Lana Graziano.
pages cm
Includes index.
"A Perigee book."
ISBN 978-0-399-16660-0
1. Cooking, Italian. 2. Mob wives. I. Graziano, Jennifer. II. Graziano, Lana. III. Title.
TX723.G7574 20114
641.5945—dc23   2013039936

First edition: February 2014

PRINTED IN THE UNITED STATES OF AMERICA

10 9 8 7 6 5 4 3 2 1

Text design by Pauline Neuwirth

The recipes contained in this book have been created for the ingredients and techniques indicated. The publisher is not responsible for your specific health or allergy needs that may require supervision. Nor is the publisher responsible for any adverse reactions you may have to the recipes contained in the book, whether you follow them as written or modify them to suit your personal dietary needs or tastes.

While the author has made every effort to provide accurate telephone numbers, Internet addresses, and other contact information at the time of publication, neither the publisher nor the author assumes any responsibility for errors, or for changes that occur after publication. Further, the publisher does not have any control over and does not assume any responsibility for author or third-party websites or their content.

Most Perigee books are available at special quantity discounts for bulk purchases for sales promotions, premiums, fund-raising, or educational use. Special books, or book excerpts, can also be created to fit specific needs. For details, write: Special.Markets@us.penguingroup.com.

We would like to dedicate this book to our parents, Anthony and Veronica Graziano, as well as our grandmother Nora Eda Amelia Cultura DiMarini Gebbia, a woman with a lot of names, a lot of spunk, and a lot of recipes. We hope you enjoy these recipes as much as we did growing up.

Veronica and Anthony Graziano, aka Mom and Dad, on family vacation

Jennifer and Grandma Nora

CONTENTS

INTRODUCTION

FOOD. WE LOVE IT. WE LIVE IT. We dream about it. We fight over it.

On the television show *Mob Wives*, where Renee is one of the stars and Jennifer is the creator and executive producer, there are many scenes centered around food. The women on the show go out to dinner to discuss what is going on in their lives, they cook for their children, they discuss sending food to their husbands who are "away," and they invite each other over for dinner parties. We caution you, however, to think twice before going over to a *Mob Wives* house for a dinner party. For one reason or another, the most conflict on the show happens during what is supposed to be a nice dinner event or a quick conversation over food. Do you remember Renee's "sit-down" dinner where an all-out brawl broke out? Or Drita's heated conversation with her husband about sending the wrong food items to prison, ending with her ripping the phone out of the wall and telling him "he shouldn't eat"? Karen and Carla, as well as Ramona and Carla, both had heated arguments over dinner, and let's not forget the brunch at Big Ang's house that had butter knives on the loose. What's wrong with this picture? It's not always bad, though: Big Ang and her son bond over the amazing meals she cooks for him, and we did see the entire clan come together, kids and all, to "bury the hatchet" over a beautiful sit-down dinner celebration in New York City at the end of Season 2. Seems to us that dinner with the *Mob Wives* mirrors dinner with the Graziano family. Just like any typical (or not so typical) Italian family, we may fight over our meals but it seems like food is the common denominator that brings us all together in the end.

Every holiday, we gathered at a family member's house to celebrate over food and drink. Everyone came over and spent time telling stories and talking over pasta, meats, salads, vegetables, good wine, and dessert. From great aunts, to grandmothers, to Mom, Dad, and cousins—we all got together and each made one of our own specialties. Recipes passed down from both Mom's and Dad's sides of the family were always enjoyed in our home. Our maternal grandmother, Nora, was the best cook and teacher. Lana, the eldest of us Graziano girls, sat at her side all day long helping her by adding a dash of this and smidgen of that. Lana honed her cooking skills over the years as she watched, took notes, and cooked side-by-side with our grandmother, mother, and even our father. Even though Dad was not the kind of guy you would expect to find in the kitchen, he was an amazing cook. We remember watching him jar his homemade caponata, marinara sauce from fresh tomatoes, and many other specialties.

Lana spent lots of time perfecting her craft until she one day opened her own restaurant, where she cooked in the kitchen herself and trained her own chefs. Speaking of restaurants, we'd also like to pay homage to a very special restaurant in our lives. Supreme Macaroni Company, located in Manhattan's Hell's Kitchen, was owned by our grandmother's sister from the late 1940s and remained in her family up until it was sold about ten years ago. Supreme Macaroni was where our father first learned to cook. He and our mother both worked there when they were fifteen and nineteen years old, respectively. Love of food spawned love of each other.

PHOTO BY MATT DOYLE

We remember visiting Supreme Macaroni many times when we were young. We hold many fond memories of this place. We used to visit Tia Suzi, Aunt Faye, and cousin Marilyn all the time, and they even let us help sell the dry macaroni in the front of the restaurant, which was an old-style *salumeria*. In fact, this is where Jennifer learned how to make one of our favorite dishes—penne alla vodka—when chef Jimmy used to let us in the kitchen all the time. We loved going there, helping out, spending time with family, and eating tortonis!

Although Supreme Macaroni Company was not owned by us, we believe this is the place that inspired our father to go into the restaurant business on his own. Soon came Villa Verona, our first family restaurant, which we opened on Staten Island after first moving there. Soon after, Dad opened A Wing and a Clam and many more, including Mama Rosa's, which was the first restaurant he opened in partnership with Lana. After that, Lana went on to open Mangiare Tu in South Jersey, which had lines waiting out the door for eight years. That's where Lana taught us all how to cook, and where Renee developed her own flair for cooking.

Restaurants are a part of our legacy, and food is in our blood. We have gathered many of these family recipes and tested them, perfecting them for the modern home cook. Included in this book are real, authentic Italian recipes—the kind that would make our grandmother proud!

Some included here are Sicilian-Style Codfish, Chicken Cutlet Parmesan, Veal Osso Buco, Lana's Meatballs, Sunday Gravy, and Italian Wedding Soup. We've also included lots of scrumptious side dishes to mix and match—Chop Meat–Stuffed Red Peppers, Stuffed Artichokes, Italian Cheesy Garlic Bread, Escarole and Beans, Sicilian Rice Balls, and much more. We hope that you enjoy making these dishes as much as we do, and that you serve them to your family with love—or else you'll have to answer to us!

— *Renee, Jennifer, and Lana Graziano*

How To Use A
Meat Cleaver

Renee crabbing at the Jersey Shore

Dad on our family boat

1

SEAFOOD

SLEEPIN' WITH THE FISHES!

Seafood and fish are among the Graziano favorites. In fact, we used to own a seafood restaurant called A Wing and a Clam. We all love to go fishing, crabbing, clamming, you name it—and did so on many of our trips to Bermuda, the Bahamas, and other islands with Mom and Dad. Dad was a champ and caught many large and small fish along the way—a hammerhead shark, a beautiful marlin, and a tremendous grouper—and even stuffed them for display in his "animal room." Fish and seafood spark our fondest childhood memories, from catching the fish to cooking it to eating it. Garlic Crabs, Zuppa Clams in Red Sauce, Shrimp Oreganata, Frutti di Mare, and Swordfish with Anchovies and Olives are only some of what we will teach you to make. We all share a love of the ocean and the food it bears—but none of us want to be fish food at the bottom of the ocean with a pair of cement shoes on!

ZUPPA DE PESCE

The traditional translation is "fish soup," but this dish is so much more than that. It's an array of flavors and a variety of fish simmered together to create a soup-like sauce. This dish can be served alone with some Italian bread for dipping or over a bed of linguine.

1 dozen mussels

1 dozen clams

3 tablespoons olive oil

1 onion, chopped

3 cloves garlic, crushed

Crushed pepper flakes (optional)

Salt and pepper, to taste

1 (16-ounce) can whole plum tomatoes

1½ pounds shrimp, cleaned, tails removed, and deveined

1½ pounds monkfish

1 pound spaghetti

With a stiff brush, scrub the mussels and clams under cold water to remove the grit. Discard any open clams or cracked clams. Soak and rinse several times until you don't see any more sand or grit. Pull all of the hair out of the mussels, pulling toward the point end.

In a 5- to 6-quart saucepan, add the olive oil, onion, garlic, crushed pepper, salt, and pepper and cook over medium heat for 4 to 5 minutes, until the garlic starts to soften and the onions become translucent. Stir in the tomatoes and their juices, and the water. Add all of the fish and bring to a boil. Simmer for 12 to 15 minutes, until shrimp are pink and shellfish have opened up.

While seafood cooks, bring a large pot of water to boil. Cook the spaghetti according to package instructions. Drain and toss with the seafood. Serve hot.

SERVES 6

ZUPPA CLAMS IN GARLIC AND OIL

Any clam recipe reminds us of our dad. When we were younger, we had a family boat—a thirty-five-foot Silverton—and Dad used to take us out every weekend. Mom was always petrified of the sea and never came with us, but she waited on the dock all day for us to return safely. We loved it. We would stop in the middle of the ocean, jump off the top of the boat, and go swimming for an hour or so. But the best part of the day was when we docked at one of our favorite restaurants in Long Island or the Jersey Shore. We would order clams and steamers by the bucket load and we all dug in, each one of us often scrambling for the last clam. We would then head back to the Staten Island boatyard, worn out from the day's activities, with a take-home bag for Mom. Our family makes clams a number of different ways, but this is one of our all-time favorite recipes.

2 dozen littleneck clams

8–10 cloves garlic, chopped into large pieces

4 tablespoons olive oil

¼ cup chicken stock

Salt and pepper, to taste

½ cup bottled clam juice

½ cup fresh parsley, chopped

With a stiff brush, scrub the clams under cold water to remove the grit. Discard any open clams or cracked clams. Soak and rinse several times until you don't see any more sand or grit.

In a 2-quart saucepan, sauté the garlic in olive oil over medium heat, then add chicken stock. Bring to a boil, and reduce heat to medium. Add salt and pepper and cook for 4 to 5 minutes. Increase heat to high and add the clam juice, clams, and parsley. Cook, covered, until clams open, then cook for additional 2 minutes.

SERVES 4 TO 6

ZUPPA CLAMS IN RED SAUCE

Zuppa is an Italian word that means soup. While the clams are delicious served alone in this delectable sauce, the dish can also be served over linguine or spaghetti. And, as every Italian knows, nothing goes better with a hearty sea soup than a loaf of brick-oven Italian bread for dipping. We serve this dish a lot on Christmas Eve. In fact, we are always elbow-deep in the juice while eating, and it's probably the only time the Graziano family is silent. All you can hear is the muffled sound of Christmas music in the background and the slurping of clams loud and clear.

2 dozen littleneck clams

8–10 cloves garlic, chopped into large pieces

4 tablespoons olive oil

¼ cup chicken stock

Salt and pepper, to taste

3 fresh plum tomatoes, cut into 4 to 6 pieces

½ cup bottled clam juice

⅓ cup fresh basil, chopped

With a stiff brush, scrub the clams under cold water to remove the grit. Discard any open clams or cracked clams. Soak and rinse several times until you don't see any more sand or grit.

In a 2-quart saucepan, sauté the garlic in olive oil over medium heat, then add chicken stock and bring to a boil. Reduce heat to medium, add salt and pepper, and cook for 4 to 5 minutes. Increase heat to high and add the tomatoes, clam juice, basil, and clams. Cook, covered, until the clams open up, then cook for 2 additional minutes.

SERVES 4 TO 6

GARLIC CRABS

We were always on one adventure or another when we were younger, and going crabbing at the Jersey Shore was one of our favorites. Renee used to put the bait in the crab cage like a champ. She would hook the fish right through the eyes, and always caught the most crabs. Then we would go home and Dad would chase us around the house with the live crabs before putting them in the pot for cooking. He made the best crabs in any style but his garlic crabs were the best.

1 dozen crabs

¼ cup olive oil

1½ heads garlic, peeled and cloves cut in half

1 cup chicken stock

2 tablespoons finely chopped fresh parsley

Salt and pepper, to taste

1 (28-ounce) can San Marzano (or your preferred brand) crushed tomatoes (optional, if you'd prefer a red sauce)

To prepare the crabs: Place your thumb under the outer edge of the top shell that's closest to you. Pry the shell off, pulling away from your body. It should come off in one piece. Flip the crab over and peel off the apron. Then peel and remove the crab's lungs and gills. You can also ask your fishmonger or butcher to prepare the crabs. Set aside.

In a 3-quart saucepan, sauté the olive oil and garlic over medium heat until slightly brown, then add the chicken stock, parsley, salt, and pepper. Add tomatoes, if using. Add crabs, stirring to coat with the sauce, and cook over a medium-high heat for 12 to 15 minutes. Stir occasionally, until crabs have turned red.

SERVES 4

GARLIC SHRIMP

As cliché as it sounds, these shrimp are finger-licking good! They don't last long on the dinner table, so you better snatch yours up fast. The best part of the whole dish is sucking the shrimp shells, which hold all the flavor and juice of the dish. One time we had to make seven pounds of this just to make sure everyone at the table had enough. This can be served with rice or over a bed of linguine with garlic and oil.

2 pounds extra-large (16/20) shrimp, shells on

4 tablespoons olive oil

2 heads garlic, peeled and chopped into large chunks

6 tablespoons (¾ stick) salted butter

Salt and pepper, to taste

½–1 teaspoon ground cayenne pepper

½ lemon

Rinse shrimp in cold water and set aside. In a sauté pan, heat the olive oil and garlic over medium heat until garlic is softened. Add butter, salt, and pepper. Add shrimp and cayenne pepper (the more you use, the hotter your dish will be). Cook the shrimp for 3 to 4 minutes, turn, and cook an additional 3 to 4 minutes. Squeeze the lemon on top, and serve hot.

SERVES 4 TO 6

SHRIMP AND CALAMARI WITH LONG HOTS

This was one of the dishes that Lana's restaurant, Mangiare Tu, was known for. It's perfectly spicy and delicious with just the right amount of garlic—an Italian-lover's dream.

¼ cup olive oil

1 head garlic (whole)

4–6 long hot peppers (whole)

1½ pounds extra-large (16/20) shrimp

1 pound calamari

½ lemon

In a frying pan over medium heat, sauté the olive oil and garlic, cooking until tender. Add long hots and cook for 15 to 20 minutes, flipping once. Once the long hots are cooked, remove and set aside. When cool, cut into 1-inch pieces, and remove the stems and seeds. In the same frying pan, add the shrimp and cook them for 3 to 4 minutes; turn, and cook for an additional 3 to 4 minutes. Add the calamari and cook together for another 5 or 6 minutes, turning them every minute. Once the fish is done, squeeze the lemon on top. Return the long hots to pan, turn off heat; and let sit for 2 or 3 minutes before serving.

SERVES 4

SHRIMP OREGANATA

This is another one of Jennifer's specialties and one of her favorite dishes. We're convinced she only likes to cook what she likes to eat! This dish was passed down to her by another great chef in our family, Dad's sister Aunt Celia. When Jenn is in a cooking bind she calls one of three people—Lana, Aunt Celia, or Big Ang! They're her three favorite cooks—other than Mom, Dad, and Grandma of course.

2 pounds (24/30) shrimp, peeled and deveined

¼ cup olive oil

8–10 cloves garlic, minced

¾ cup (1½ sticks) salted butter, divided

Salt and pepper, to taste

2 tablespoons fresh basil, chopped

¼ cup chicken stock

¾ cup seasoned bread crumbs

½ lemon

Preheat oven to 350F. Grease a 9 × 13-inch baking pan, and set aside.

Rinse shrimp and set aside. In a sauté pan, cook olive oil and garlic over medium heat and cook until garlic is softened, about 4 minutes. Add 1 stick butter, salt, pepper, basil, and chicken stock. Cook for another 1 to 2 minutes, and then add the bread crumbs to absorb the juice and form a thick paste.

Place the shrimp on the bottom of prepared baking pan and spoon the bread crumb mixture evenly over each shrimp. Using remaining ½ stick butter, place a small dab of butter on every third or fourth shrimp, and then squeeze the lemon on top. Bake for 10 to 12 minutes, until the shrimp are pink.

SERVES 4 TO 6

FRUTTI DI MARE

This is one of the family's favorite dishes. When making it for Dad, we include scungilli because he loves it so much, but it can be made with or without it. We love eating this on the second day because it tastes even better when all the juices marinate! It's a great New Year's Eve dish, and we would look forward to this every year. It is a tradition, and we even made sure to have it the year we spent New Year's in the Bahamas—except that time we added in conch that Dad handpicked right from the ocean off the docks in Nassau. The funniest part was when he leaned over too far and fell right in the water.

1 pound calamari, with tentacles cleaned

¾ pound (16/20) shrimp, peeled and deveined

1 pound lobster meat, cut up into bite-size pieces

¾ cup olive oil

4 celery stalks, diced

1 teaspoon finely chopped fresh parsley

2 cloves garlic, finely diced

Salt and pepper, to taste

1½–2 lemons

Rinse the calamari in a colander under cold water. Separate the tubes from the tentacles, and cut the tubes into rings. Bring two large pots of water to boil. Put the tubes in one pot, and put the tentacles in another. Cook them both for 5 minutes, drain, and rinse both under cold water. Set aside.

Clean the pots, refill with water, and bring to a boil. Add the shrimp to one pot and the lobster to the other. Cook the shrimp for 5 to 6 minutes and the lobster for 7 to 8 minutes. Drain and rinse under cold water. Set aside.

In a large bowl, add the olive oil, celery, parsley, garlic, and salt and pepper to taste and mix well. Add all of the fish to the mix, toss, and squeeze the lemon on top. Toss well. Best served at room temperature.

SERVES 4 TO 6

SICILIAN-STYLE CODFISH

Another word for this is baccala, *but in the Italian community* baccala *is also meant as an insult—but we won't get into too much detail with that. So the next time you're making this dish, think about all of the people that you think are a real* baccala!

4–6 cod fillets

6 tablespoons olive oil, divided

Juice of 1½ lemons (about ⅓ cup)

Salt and pepper, to taste

1–2 anchovy fillets

1 teaspoon salted capers, rinsed

3 tablespoons finely chopped fresh parsley

Wash the cod fillets under cold water and place them on a plate. Combine 3 tablespoons olive oil and half of the lemon juice in a bowl and dip the fillets in the mixture. Sprinkle some salt and pepper over each fillet. Put them on a flat dish and let them marinate for 1 hour.

Preheat oven to 350F.

In a sauté pan, melt anchovy fillet(s) and the capers with remaining 3 tablespoons olive oil over low heat for 10 to 15 minutes. Place the cod fillets on a baking sheet, and evenly divide anchovy mixture among tops of each fillet. Add parsley and remaining lemon juice. Cover with foil and cook, covered, for 30 minutes. Remove foil and cook for another 10 minutes, until fish is very white in color and flakes easily.

SERVES 4 TO 6

SWORDFISH WITH ANCHOVIES AND OLIVES

Our Grandma Nora is from the old country, where swordfish was such a staple in the diet of the people. Grandma Nora looked forward to any chance she could possibly get to have a taste of home, and the entire family reaped the benefits of one of the tastiest kinds of fish there is.

4 pieces swordfish, cut into palm-sized pieces

6 tablespoons olive oil, divided

2 spring onions, chopped

2 cloves garlic, chopped

20 salted capers, rinsed

8 black olives, chopped

Pinch crushed red pepper flakes

2 anchovy fillets

1 cup white wine

8 fresh plum tomatoes, chopped

Salt and pepper, to taste

1 tablespoon parsley, chopped

Place the swordfish pieces in a large bowl with 3 tablespoons olive oil and set aside. In a sauté pan on medium heat, add remaining 3 tablespoons olive oil, as well onion, garlic, capers, olives, red pepper flakes, and anchovy fillets. Stir until the anchovies melt into the oil and the onion becomes translucent, about 5 minutes.

Place the chunks of swordfish in the pan and slowly add the white wine. Cook on medium-high heat until the alcohol is burned off, 3 to 4 minutes. Lower the heat and add the tomatoes, salt, and pepper, stirring without breaking up the swordfish, and cover. Simmer for 30 minutes, until done. When ready to serve, sprinkle with parsley.

SERVES 4

TUNA WITH TOMATOES AND ONIONS

We love this very light, spring dish. If you're looking to dine al fresco, this would be the dish to do it with. It's delicious and a great meal to have while you're trying to work for that beach body in anticipation of the upcoming summer months. Mom always made this on hot summer days, and we sat in the yard to eat this and other seafood dishes.

4 tuna steaks

Salt and pepper, to taste

6 tablespoons olive oil, divided

3 cloves garlic, diced

1 large sweet onion, cut in slices

1 teaspoon salted capers, rinsed

6 fresh plum tomatoes, diced

¼ cup chicken stock

2 tablespoons fresh parsley

Place the tuna steaks on a large plate and sprinkle with salt and pepper; set aside. In a sauté pan, heat 3 tablespoons olive oil over medium heat. Add garlic, onion, and capers, and cook for 10 minutes. Add the tomatoes, chicken stock, and parsley. Cook, stirring occasionally, for 5 minutes, then turn off heat.

In a frying pan, heat remaining 3 tablespoons olive oil over medium heat, and pan-sear the tuna steaks on each side for 3 minutes for medium-rare (if you like your tuna cooked well, cook for 5 minutes per side). Top each tuna steak with tomato mixture, and serve.

SERVES 4

BROILED FILLET OF SOLE OREGANATA

As we all know, Renee has had many arguments with the girls on Mob Wives—even some whom she loves very much. She has been known to say she would like to "fillet her like a fish," but mostly she gets along well with others. This dish is one we love because, if you notice, we love anything "oreganata." The bread crumbs, the garlic . . . it's all amazing! This dish is the perfect combination of a white, flaky fish with just the right amount of bread crumbs to keep it light.

1 cup seasoned bread crumbs

3 tablespoons grated Pecorino-Romano cheese

6 basil leaves, chopped

Salt and pepper, to taste

1 lemon

1 pound fresh sole or flounder fillet

¼ cup olive oil

3–4 tablespoons salted butter

Preheat oven to 375F.

In a bowl mix the bread crumbs, grated cheese, basil, salt, and pepper and squeeze the lemon onto the mixture. Wash each fillet and pat dry. Using a brush spread some olive oil on each fillet. Place the fillets in large baking dish. With your hands, evenly spread the bread crumb mixture over fillets, and top each with a thin slice of butter. Bake for 20 to 25 minutes, until fish flakes easily.

SERVES 4

LOBSTER ARRAGIATTA

This dish is also called "Angry Lobster," by some and it's very fitting for Renee's persona on Mob Wives. *There are times when she got so angry with the women that we almost felt she wanted them to "sleep with the fishes." Then she thought about it and realized she had nothing to be angry about . . . none of them can cook as well as she can. And certainly no one can crack open a lobster with their teeth like Renee, either!*

1 pound linguine

4 live lobsters

2 cups flour

2 tablespoons ground
cayenne pepper

1 cup olive oil

2 heads garlic
(or more, if you like garlic)

2½ cups chicken stock, divided

10–12 fresh
basil leaves, chopped

Salt and pepper, to taste

Bring a large pot of water to boil. Cook pasta al dente according to package instructions, drain, and set aside.

Prepare the lobsters: cut the live lobsters down the middle and take out the sacs, but leave the eggs and roe inside. Cut the tail into two pieces and crack the claws in half, dripping the juices into a pan. Separate the two halves of the body. All together, you should have 4 to 6 pieces of lobster with the shells intact. You can also ask your fishmonger or butcher to prepare the lobsters for you.

Combine the flour and cayenne pepper in a large bowl. Dip lobster pieces into the mixture, leaving the shells on. Coat lightly and shake off the excess flour.

Preheat oven to 350F.

In a 4-quart saucepan, heat olive oil over medium-high heat and add the garlic. Cook until the garlic is golden brown. Add about half the chicken stock, and slowly add the lobster pieces. Brown the lobster on each side for 3 to 4 minutes (don't overcook them), and transfer to a cookie sheet. Place in the oven and bake for 10 minutes, and then place under the broiler for another 2 to 3 minutes. Slowly add more of the chicken stock to the saucepan used to cook the lobster, and add pasta to coat and absorb the sauce. Once the pasta is coated with the sauce, transfer to a serving bowl, and top with some lobster pieces for presentation. Place remaining lobster in a separate bowl for serving.

SERVES 4

BAKED SALMON

Salmon is a fish we very rarely ate growing up—except for our mom always putting it out for bagels. But one day, Mom made this very simple salmon dish and we all loved it. It was light, but extremely tasty. This is a very simple way to make salmon on a hot summer day. It's perfect served with a vegetable side dish, and we also like to enjoy it with a cold bottle of our white wine.

4 pieces salmon fillet

2 cloves garlic, minced

2–3 tablespoons fresh lemon juice

Salt and pepper, to taste

1 teaspoon chopped fresh basil

3 tablespoons olive oil

4 tablespoons butter

Preheat oven to 375F. Grease a baking dish large enough to hold salmon fillets in a single layer.

Place the salmon in prepared dish. In a medium bowl, combine the garlic, lemon juice, salt, pepper, and basil. Drizzle olive oil over the salmon and add the garlic/lemon mixture. Top each fillet with a pat of butter.

Roast salmon for 20 to 25 minutes, or until it flakes easily with a fork.

SERVES 4

Renee, Jennifer, and Lana Graziano

Top: Anthony, Veronica, and Jennifer
Bottom: Renee and Lana

PASTA

WE'LL MAKE YOU A PASTA YOU CAN'T REFUSE

Pasta and Italians go hand in hand. There's not an Italian alive who doesn't enjoy a good, old-fashioned dish of macaroni. From penne to rigatoni, spaghetti, linguine, fusilli, orecchiette, ziti, lasagna, rotini, and more—there are so many delicious variations of pasta and sauces in the Italian cuisine that we would need to dedicate a whole book to pasta alone. In this case, we have chosen some traditional Italian pasta dishes as well as some of our personal favorites to share with you. Everything from Linguine with Clam Sauce—both red and white—to Baked Ziti, Penne alla Vodka, and Sunday Gravy are included in this section. Now, go cook and enjoy—and that's not a suggestion, that's an order!

A little pasta tip: Take the lid from the top of one of the tomato cans and put it on top of the burner and then set your pot on top of it. This prevents the meat and sauce from burning on the bottom of the pot. Try it!

LINGUINE WITH RED CLAM SAUCE

Dad was born and raised in New York City's East Village, so it was only natural for him to go back and open up a restaurant in his "hometown." A Wing and a Clam opened on 1st Avenue and 13th Street in Manhattan in the late 1970s, and this was one of the dishes most ordered from the menu. Dad made it so delicious, and most of his friends liked to add a little red pepper on top after it was served to make it extra hot and spicy. We remember being young kids and sitting at the table with all of these burly men, slurping down clams and sauce and usually ending up with most of it on their shirts!

2½–3 dozen littleneck clams

3 tablespoons extra virgin olive oil

10 cloves garlic, chopped

2 tablespoons butter

1 (28-ounce) can whole Italian tomatoes

Salt and pepper, to taste

Crushed red pepper flakes, to taste

1 (8-ounce) bottle clam juice

4 tablespoons finely chopped basil

1 pound linguine

With a stiff brush, scrub the clams under cold water to remove the grit. Discard any open clams or cracked clams. Soak and rinse several times until you don't see any more sand or grit.

In a 3-quart saucepan set over medium heat, add the olive oil and garlic. Sauté until the garlic is softened. Add the butter and tomatoes, crushing them with your hands, and then add the juices from the tomatoes. Add the salt, pepper, and red pepper flakes, and bring to a boil. Add the clam juice and basil, and bring to a boil for 1 to 2 minutes, then reduce heat to simmer the sauce for 30 to 40 minutes. Add the clams to the sauce, and boil until the clams open. Simmer for 5 to 7 minutes.

Bring a large pot of water to boil. Cook the pasta according to package instructions, drain, and toss with the clams to serve.

SERVES 4 TO 6

LINGUINE WITH WHITE CLAM SAUCE

This is the dish we like to consider Italian soul food. You'll notice it's on the menu at most Italian restaurants, and even the novice Italian eater loves it. The more clams, the better! This can also be served with a little red pepper on top for those who like things spicy, or even with some grated cheese. After you make and eat this dish, you'll understand why the old-timers order this more than anything when out at a restaurant. Linguine and white clams is better than chicken soup for the soul.

2½–3 dozen littleneck clams

3 tablespoons extra virgin olive oil

2 tablespoons butter

10 cloves garlic, chopped

1 cup chicken stock

1 (8-ounce) bottle clam juice

4 tablespoons very finely chopped parsley

Salt and pepper, to taste

Crushed red pepper flakes, to taste

1 pound linguine

With a stiff brush, scrub the clams under cold water to remove the grit. Discard any open clams or cracked clams. Soak and rinse the clams in cold water several times, until you don't see any more sand or grit.

In a 3-quart saucepan, add the olive oil, butter, and garlic over medium heat, and sauté until garlic is softened. Add the chicken stock and clam juice. Increase heat to high, bring to a boil, and cook for 10 minutes. Reduce heat to a simmer. Add the parsley, salt, pepper, and red pepper flakes, and cook for 30 to 40 minutes. Add clams to the sauce, and boil until clams open, then simmer for 5 to 7 minutes.

Bring a large pot of water to boil. Cook the pasta according to package instructions, drain, and toss everything together to serve.

SERVES 4 TO 6

LINGUINE CARBONARA

This is a hearty Italian dish, and boy, is it delicious! If you like pancetta drowned in a cream sauce, you're going to love this recipe. It's the pasta that's known to stick to your ribs. "You're gonna get chubby," was our mother's mantra when we all went for seconds!

1 pound linguine

2 tablespoons olive oil

1 small sweet onion, cut into small dice

Salt and pepper, to taste

¾ cup pancetta, cubed

6 egg yolks, beaten

1 cup light cream

¾ cup grated Pecorino-Romano cheese

Bring a large pot of water to boil. Cook pasta al dente (6 to 8 minutes), drain, and set aside. In a sauté pan, combine olive oil, onion, salt, and pepper. Sauté until onions are translucent, about 5 minutes, and then add the pancetta. Mix the egg yolks, cream, and cheese together in a separate bowl. Add the cooked pasta to the pan with the pancetta and onions. Slowly add egg yolk mixture until the sauce thickens.

SERVES 4 TO 6

SPAGHETTI WITH PESTO SAUCE

Growing up, we never understood why "leaves" were so important in all of Grandma's dishes. She would go to the farmers' market and pick the best leaves off of the basil plant. Then she would take them and throw them into the blender and make the perfect pesto. Not only were we surprised how good this sauce was but the fact that it was uncooked and so easy to make was really a treat!

1 pound spaghetti

⅓ cup olive oil

2 cloves garlic

Salt and pepper, to taste

¼ cup grated Pecorino-Romano cheese

2 bunches fresh basil, leaves removed from stems

½ teaspoon crushed red pepper flakes

½ cup (1 stick) salted butter, softened

Bring a large pot of water to boil. Cook spaghetti according to package instructions, and reserve about ¼ cup cooking water. Set aside. Combine the rest of the ingredients in a blender, and add the reserved pasta cooking water to the blender to loosen the mixture. Blend the ingredients again, and toss with the cooked spaghetti in a large bowl.

SERVES 4 TO 6

BAKED ZITI

Renee made a baked ziti on Mob Wives *once, but no one ate a bite and not because it wasn't delicious. They were too busy having a "sit-down" dinner that evening over an issue Renee was having with Carla. Boy, they didn't know what they were missing but audience members certainly got a mouthful of good old-fashioned* Mob Wives *drama!*

1 pound ziti

2 cloves garlic, minced

3 tablespoons olive oil

1 onion, diced

2 (28-ounce) cans San Marzano crushed tomatoes

1 pound fresh ricotta, drained

Salt and pepper, to taste

10–12 fresh basil leaves, chopped

2 egg yolks

1 pound whole-milk mozzarella, cut into 1-inch cubes, divided

½ cup grated Pecorino-Romano cheese, divided

Bring a large pot of salted water to boil and add the ziti. Cook until just al dente, 8 to 10 minutes; drain and set aside. Heat olive oil in a 3-quart saucepan over medium-high heat and sauté the garlic. Add onion and sauté for 4 to 5 minutes until translucent. Add tomatoes and continue to cook over medium-high heat until the sauce boils. Lower the heat and simmer the sauce for 2 hours.

Preheat oven to 400F.

In a large bowl, mix the ricotta, salt and pepper, basil, and egg yolks. Add the ziti and stir to coat pasta. Spread ½ cup sauce in the bottom of a 15 × 10-inch glass baking dish. Layer half of the ziti on top of the sauce. Sprinkle with half the mozzarella cubes and half of the grated cheese. Pour 2 cups sauce over the cheese, and spread in an even layer. Top with remaining pasta, and spread 1 cup sauce over pasta. Sprinkle with the remaining cheeses, and place some sauce on top. Place the dish in the oven and bake, uncovered, until browned and bubbly, 45 minutes to 1 hour. Let rest for 5 minutes before cutting.

SERVES 4 TO 6

ORECCHIETTE WITH SAUSAGE AND BROCCOLI RABE

This is a dish we picked up later in our lives, deriving our inspiration from Big Ang, who makes it the best! Orecchiette is our personal choice for pasta, as the curves holds the juices so perfectly. The combination of the sausage and broccoli rabe along with the pasta leaves your mouth watering for more.

1 pound orecchiette

⅓ cup olive oil

6 large cloves garlic, minced

½ pound Italian sweet or hot sausage, cut into 1-inch rounds

Salt and pepper, to taste

Pinch crushed red pepper flakes

1½ cups chicken stock

1½ pounds broccoli rabe, trimmed

½ cup grated Pecorino-Romano or Parmigiano-Reggiano cheese

Bring a large pot of water to boil. Cook pasta according to package directions until al dente. Drain and set aside. Heat olive oil in a frying pan over medium-low heat, and sauté garlic until softened. Add sausage, salt, pepper, and red pepper flakes and cook, stirring and breaking up the sausage with a wooden spoon until browned, about 7 minutes. Add the chicken stock. Bring to a boil, add the broccoli rabe, and stir to combine. Cook until the broccoli rabe is tender, 6 to 8 minutes. Add the pasta to the frying pan and stir to combine. Add cheese, to taste.

SERVES 4

PARMIGIANO-BAKED RIGATONI WITH CAULIFLOWER, PEAS, AND PROSCIUTTO

This is not your typical baked macaroni dish. The combination of ingredients sets your palate on fire in this Northern Italian specialty. Believe it or not, the kids really love this and with just the right amount of prosciutto, it's really an Italian-lover's dream.

1 pound rigatoni

1 large head cauliflower, cut into 1-inch florets

3½ tablespoons olive oil, divided

3–4 cloves garlic, chopped

1½ cups heavy cream

Salt and pepper, to taste

4 ounces sliced prosciutto, cut into thick strips

½ (12-ounce) package frozen sweet peas

½ cup panko bread crumbs

½ cup grated Parmigiano-Reggiano cheese

½ cup seasoned bread crumbs

½ tablespoon finely chopped fresh rosemary

Bring a large pot of water to a boil. Cook the rigatoni until al dente (8 to 10 minutes); before the rigatoni is done, add the cauliflower florets to the pot. Drain and set aside. In the same pot, heat 1 tablespoon olive oil over medium heat and add garlic. Cook for 1 minute until lightly golden. Add cream and simmer until slightly thickened, about 2 minutes. Season with salt and pepper to taste.

Return the rigatoni and cauliflower to the pot. Add the prosciutto and peas and cook for 2 to 3 minutes to coat and warm through, stirring occasionally. Turn oven to broil. In a medium bowl, toss the panko, grated cheese, bread crumbs, rosemary, and remaining 2½ tablespoons olive oil. Season with salt and pepper. Transfer pasta to a large shallow baking dish and sprinkle the panko mixture evenly over the top. Broil for 2 to 4 minutes, until the topping is evenly browned.

SERVES 4 TO 6

PASTA FAGIOLI

This is a classic Italian soup, and even more popular than Italian wedding soup. Our kids all loved this soup for breakfast, lunch, and dinner—literally. Lana's eldest daughter, Michelle, sometimes a picky eater as a child, was even a fan of it, too. She especially loved it when sautéed escarole was added to the pot.

1 pound ditalini pasta

3 tablespoons olive oil

1 large sweet onion

Salt and pepper, to taste

8 fresh plum tomatoes, diced

3 celery stalks, diced

2 (14-ounce) cans chicken broth

1 cup water

1 (15.5-ounce) can cannellini beans, drained and rinsed

Grated Pecorino-Romano cheese, to taste

Bring a large pot of water to boil. Cook pasta according to package instructions, and set aside. Heat olive oil in a 3-quart saucepan over medium heat, and sauté onion until translucent. Add salt and pepper, to taste. Add tomatoes and cook for 10 to 15 minutes. Add celery, chicken stock, and water, and cook for another 45 minutes. Add the beans and cook for an additional 15 minutes.

To serve: Set out 4 to 6 bowls. Add a little pasta to each and top with a scoop of the soup and a sprinkle of grated cheese. You can add more pasta or more soup to your liking. Enjoy!

SERVES 4 TO 6

PASTA WITH CANNELLINI BEANS AND CAULIFLOWER

This is not a meal to be taken lightly—no pun intended. This is Lana's daughter Sonni's favorite pasta dish. When she was younger, she would eat each bean individually so that all that was left was the macaroni and cauliflower. Now she eats at least two bowls or more.

1 pound small pasta shells (or any pasta you like)

4 tablespoons olive oil

6–8 cloves garlic

6 fresh plum tomatoes, diced

1½ cups chicken stock, divided

½ teaspoon crushed red pepper flakes

Salt and pepper, to taste

1 head cauliflower, cut into florets

1 (28-ounce) can cannellini beans

Bring a large pot of water to boil. Cook pasta according to package instructions, drain, and set aside. Heat olive oil in a 3-quart saucepan over medium-high heat and sauté garlic until slightly golden brown. Reduce heat to medium, add tomatoes, and cook for 5 to 6 minutes. Add ¾ cup of the chicken stock, crushed red pepper, salt, and pepper. Increase heat to high and bring the mixture to a boil; add the cauliflower. Reduce heat to a simmer, add the cannellini beans, and cook for another 30 minutes. Add the pasta to the pot and toss to coat thoroughly.

SERVES 4 TO 6

SPAGHETTI WITH PUTTANESCA SAUCE

This dish is Renee's absolute favorite because Grandma used to make it special just for her. It's the most delicious thing ever, and it's the only recipe with sardines in it that Renee would eat because it was so good. Restaurant-style puttanesca never measured up to Grandma's! With this recipe, you will have some extra sauce to use any way you'd like.

3 tablespoons olive oil

2–3 cloves garlic, minced

1 onion, chopped

2 (28-ounce) cans San Marzano tomatoes, crushed

6 black olives

6 green olives

1 (5-ounce) can Italian tuna

1 teaspoon baby capers

2 tablespoons fresh parsley

Fresh pepper, to taste

1 pound spaghetti

Heat olive oil in a large frying pan over medium heat, and sauté garlic and onion until softened. Add tomatoes, and cook over medium-high heat for 10 minutes. Reduce heat to medium-low and cook the sauce for another 30 minutes. Stir in remaining ingredients, and cook for another 45 minutes.

Bring a large pot of water to boil. Cook spaghetti according to package instructions, drain, and top with sauce to serve.

SERVES 4 TO 6

PENNE ALLA VODKA

Penne alla vodka is a dish that gained popularity in the 1990s, and it quickly became one of our favorites. Some like it with a lot of cream, which will make it a pretty pink color, and others prefer a touch of cream, which will make it more of a salmon color. Either way, this dish is a staple at all of our family parties (particularly because of the vodka)—whether a backyard affair, birthday, or a holiday. Renee was never much of a drinker and often preferred to omit the vodka, but we liked to put in a little extra, hoping that it would knock her out for the evening! This dish can be made with a variation of pastas, but penne or rigatoni is best. If you prefer, you can add additional ingredients such as chicken or shrimp, or make it even tastier with prosciutto and peas. Either way, we hope you enjoy.

1 pound penne

3 tablespoons olive oil

1 large onion, chopped

4 cloves garlic, chopped

Salt and pepper, to taste

½ teaspoon crushed red pepper flakes

2 (28-ounce) cans San Marzano crushed tomatoes

¼ cup vodka

½ cup heavy cream

1 tablespoon butter

1 cup grated Parmigiano-Reggiano cheese

Bring a large pot of water to a boil. Cook penne according to package instructions, drain, and set aside. In a large saucepan over medium-high heat, heat olive oil and sauté the onion and garlic. Season with salt, pepper, and crushed red pepper. Cook, stirring occasionally, until the onion is soft, about 10 minutes. Add the tomatoes. Bring to a boil, reduce heat, and simmer, stirring occasionally, for another 40 minutes.

Add the vodka to the tomato mixture, and continue cooking another 10 to 15 minutes. Stir in the cream and the butter and cook for 10 more minutes. Turn off the heat.

In a pasta bowl, add 2 cups sauce and toss with the pasta and ¾ cup grated cheese. Sprinkle with remaining cheese.

SERVES 4 TO 6

SICILIAN PASTA CON SARDE
(AKA ST. JOSEPH'S DISH)

Making this dish on St. Joseph's day is an Italian tradition. Sicilians often regard St. Joseph as their patron saint, and the celebration named in his honor falls on March 19. On this day, Sicilians give thanks to St. Joseph for preventing a famine during the Middle Ages. According to legend, there was a severe drought and the people prayed to their patron saint to bring them rain. The rain did come, and the people now prepare a large feast in honor of St. Joseph every year. Typically the feast day falls during Lent and meatless dishes are prepared in honor of St. Joseph. It is a religious requirement in our household to have this dish, and to not have it on this day would be blasphemy.

¼ cup plus 1 teaspoon olive oil, divided

4 cloves garlic, minced

¼ cup chopped fennel

¼ cup diced celery

1 (28-ounce) can peeled San Marzano Italian tomatoes

3 tablespoons tomato paste

¼ cup raisins (optional)

¼ cup red wine

¼ cup pine nuts, slightly toasted

1 (3.75-ounce) can sardines in olive oil

1 teaspoon crushed fennel seeds

2 teaspoons sugar

Salt and pepper, to taste

1 tablespoon fresh parsley, chopped

1½ cups plain bread crumbs

1 pound pappardelle pasta

To make sauce: In a large pot, heat 1 teaspoon olive oil over medium heat. Sauté garlic, chopped fennel, and celery for 2 minutes. Add tomatoes and their juices and tomato paste. Cook, stirring to break up tomatoes, about 20 minutes. Reduce heat to low, and add raisins, wine, pine nuts, sardines, fennel seeds, sugar, salt, and pepper. Cook for at least 40 minutes. Stir in parsley and simmer for 10 minutes more.

To make bread crumbs: Toast bread crumbs in remaining ¼ cup olive oil in a frying pan set over low heat. Stir constantly to prevent burning. Remove from heat and set aside.

Bring a large pot of water to boil. Cook pasta according to package directions, drain, and toss with sauce. Sprinkle with bread crumbs and serve immediately.

SERVES 4 TO 6

PENNE WITH FRIED EGGPLANT

Eggplant is another vegetable that we all love. We discovered this particular dish by accident, however. Lana's eldest son, Anthony, made this for dinner one night by combining the two dishes we prepared separately—penne and perfectly fried pieces of eggplant. His discovery was amazing, and the combination just melts in your mouth!

¼ cup olive oil

4 cloves garlic

1 medium-sized eggplant, cut into 1½-inch slices and then into cubes

6–7 fresh basil leaves

2 (28-ounce) cans San Marzano plum tomatoes

Salt and pepper, to taste

½ teaspoon crushed red pepper flakes

1 pound penne pasta

½ cup ricotta salata

Heat olive oil in a large sauté pan over medium-high heat. Cook garlic until golden brown. Add eggplant and cook 4 to 5 minutes, until brown. Add basil and tomatoes, squeezing tomatoes with your hands to smash them up so the juice gets into the pan. Increase heat to high and cook until the sauce boils. Reduce heat, add salt, pepper, and crushed red pepper flakes, and simmer for 30 to 35 minutes.

In the meantime, boil a large pot of water and cook pasta according to package instructions. Drain, place in a serving bowl, and toss with the sauce. Top with the ricotta salata.

SERVES 4 TO 6

SPAGHETTI WITH ZUCCHINI AND SWEET ONION SAUCE

There's nothing like zucchini and onions! Grandma had a couple of favorite things, and zucchini was definitely one of them. It was probably one of the first words she taught baby Jennifer how to say. When Grandma babysat Jennifer, she would give her a whole zucchini to play with in the high chair. We could never figure out why this vegetable was able to quiet a fussing baby, but what we do know is that it certainly became one of Jennifer's favorites as an adult.

1½ pounds spaghetti

½ cup olive oil

6 large Vidalia onions, sliced

2 cups chicken stock, divided

Salt and pepper, to taste

4 (28-ounce) cans crushed San Marzano tomatoes

4–5 medium zucchini, peeled in strips, sliced lengthwise, then cut into 1-inch pieces

4–5 fresh basil leaves, chopped

¼ grated Pecorino-Romano cheese

In a 2-quart pot, cook the spaghetti according to package instructions and set aside. In a 3- or 4-quart pot over medium heat, heat the olive oil and add the onion, stirring until translucent. While the onions are cooking, add 1 cup chicken stock and salt and pepper. After the onions are cooked, add the tomatoes and cook over medium-high heat until the sauce boils. Let it boil for 5 minutes, then reduce heat and simmer for 1 hour. Add remaining 1 cup chicken stock, zucchini, and basil. Cover and cook for 20 minutes. Uncover, and add the grated cheese, stirring so that the cheese melts into the sauce, and cook another 15 to 20 minutes. Add 3 or 4 cups sauce to the spaghetti. Serve in pasta bowls and add more sauce and grated cheese to taste.

SERVES 4 TO 6

SUNDAY GRAVY

For most Italians, Sundays are reserved for God and family. It's a day to go to church and then have everyone over for dinner, which on this day is typically served earlier. In our house we never ate later than 4:00 p.m. on a Sunday. Mom, Dad, or Lana would take turns making the sauce each week until Jennifer and Renee got older and starting pitching in. Some people call it sauce and some people call it gravy. What many people don't know is that when Jennifer was first creating the show Mob Wives, *part of the sizzle reel used to sell the show contained a heated debate over which is correct—Sunday Sauce or Sunday Gravy. Renee contends gravy is what goes over mashed potatoes! Italians have been calling it both for years but, either way, our family makes it delicious.*

3 tablespoons olive oil

2 cloves garlic, minced

1 large sweet onion

2½ pounds country-style pork spare ribs

3 hot sausage links

3 sweet sausage links

6 (28-ounce) cans San Marzano crushed tomatoes

1 cup chicken stock

Salt and pepper, to taste

1 teaspoon crushed red pepper flakes

1½ cups grated Pecorino-Romano cheese, plus extra for sprinkling

10 fresh basil leaves, minced

1 batch Lana's Meatballs (page 139)

2 pounds pasta of your choice

In an 8-quart pot, heat olive oil over medium-high heat and add the garlic and onions. Gently stir, and then add the ribs, browning them on each side. Add the sausage and do the same. Once the meat is browned, slowly add the cans of tomatoes and the chicken stock. Add the seasonings, as well as the grated cheese and the fresh basil.

Bring sauce to a boil and let boil for 5 or 6 minutes, then reduce heat to medium-low and simmer for 3 hours. Add the meatballs and cook for an additional 2 hours.

Bring a large pot of water to boil. Cook pasta according to package instructions, drain, and serve with the meatballs and sauce.

SERVES 8 TO 10

Dad in his chef's coat, cooking at Mangiare Tu

Christmas party at Jenn's—
Jennifer, Aunt Celia, Mom, Lana, and Renee

3

BEEF

YOU GOT A BEEF WITH US?

In the mob world, when someone "has a beef" it means they have a problem, an issue, something that needs straightening out. We guarantee you, however, that you won't have any problems with our recipes in this chapter. And the only "sit-down" you will have will be at your dinner table, enjoying the feasts we are about to present to you. Beef Scallopini, Stuffed Filet Mignon, Beef Stew, and Our Traditional Meat Loaf are only a few that will have you begging for more.

STUFFED FILET MIGNON

Lana likes to stuff all of her meats and this one is by far our favorite. The succulent meat of a filet mignon, coupled with the richness of the stuffing, makes it all the more better. (As a bonus, Lana gets to cut this kind of meat right down the middle, which helps her get out some of her unwanted aggression.) Jennifer likes to brag about this dish to her friends, and she makes it whenever she throws a party. The steak should be well-done on the ends for those who like it cooked through, and red and juicy in the middle for the medium-rare lovers!

1 (4–6 pound) beef tenderloin

2 tablespoons olive oil

2 tablespoons butter

¼ cup chicken stock

1½ cups seasoned bread crumbs

½ cup grated Pecorino-Romano cheese

½ cup fresh basil, chopped

Salt and pepper, to taste

1 (8-ounce) bag shredded mozzarella cheese

Preheat oven to 425F.

Cut the tenderloin down the middle, but not all the way through, and set aside. In a sauté pan, heat the olive oil and butter over medium heat. Slowly add chicken stock, then slowly start to add the bread crumbs, cheese, basil, salt, and pepper. Toss to combine. Cook, stirring, until the liquid has evaporated. Add mozzarella cheese, stir, and remove from heat. Allow mixture to cool slightly.

Place the meat in a large baking pan. Stuff the meat with the stuffing and tie with kitchen twine at the middle and both ends. Cook for 8 to 10 minutes per pound for medium-rare meat; 10 minutes for medium; 12 minutes for medium-well.

SERVES 4 TO 6

BEEF SCALLOPINI

During the holidays, we make this delicious treasure to complement the rest of our feast. This is a very special item on our holiday menu for two reasons: One is that it's Renee's son, AJ's, favorite dish; the other is that he even joins in on helping us make it! We love the conversations we have when we prepare recipes together with the kids.

4 tablespoons olive oil, divided

4 cloves garlic, minced

5 cups fresh baby spinach

2½ pounds beef cutlets

2 eggs

1 tablespoon milk

Salt and pepper, to taste

1 cup seasoned bread crumbs

6–8 slices mozzarella cheese

¼ cup grated Parmigiano-Reggiano cheese

2 tablespoons butter

3–4 fresh plum tomatoes, chopped

½ cup Marsala wine

2 tablespoons chopped fresh basil

Preheat oven to 325F.

In a frying pan, heat 2 tablespoons olive oil and the garlic and add the spinach. Cook for 6 to 8 minutes, and set aside to cool. Place beef cutlets between pieces of plastic wrap and pound with a mallet to ⅛-inch thickness. In a bowl, mix the eggs and milk with salt and pepper to taste. Place the bread crumbs in a shallow dish. First dip the beef in the egg wash, and then dip the beef into the bread crumb mix. Gently press the beef into the bread crumbs, shaking off excess. Lay each piece of beef flat on a cutting board and place a spoonful of the spinach mixture, a slice of mozzarella, and some grated cheese on each. Roll them up and stick a toothpick on each end to hold them together.

Heat remaining 2 tablespoons olive oil and the butter in a large frying pan over medium-high heat. Fry the beef rolls in batches until just browned, 3 to 5 minutes on each side. Transfer the beef to a large baking dish. Pour the tomatoes and Marsala wine over beef and sprinkle with remaining grated cheese and basil. Bake the beef for 30 minutes, until no longer pink in the center.

SERVES 4 TO 6

CALF'S LIVER AND ONIONS IN BALSAMIC VINEGAR

Our aunt Marilyn has a very dry sense of humor. She would always tell us that the liver in this dish was cut from someone's body, but not to worry because the onions killed the human taste. We love it, but Jennifer would always cry every time Mom served this dish, she would literally be forced to eat it.

3 eggs

2 tablespoons milk

Salt and pepper, to taste

2 cups seasoned bread crumbs

3 pounds calf's liver, thinly sliced

¾ cup vegetable oil

3 tablespoons olive oil

3 large sweet onions, thinly sliced

½ cup balsamic vinegar

Preheat oven to 350F.

In a small bowl, mix the eggs and milk with the salt and pepper. Place the bread crumbs in a separate bowl. Dip the liver slices in the egg mixture, and then dredge them in the bread crumbs, making sure to cover fully. In a frying pan, heat the vegetable oil over medium heat until it bubbles. Fry cutlets about 6 minutes per side, until browned. Place them on a paper towel–lined to absorb the excess oil.

In another frying pan, heat the olive oil over medium heat and add the onion, cooking until translucent. Transfer onion to a 9 × 13-inch baking dish, and place liver on top of the onions. Sprinkle the vinegar on top of the liver, evenly over all the pieces. Put baking dish into the oven and bake, uncovered, for 12 to 15 minutes.

SERVES 6

GRILLED FLANK STEAK WITH ARUGULA, WHITE BEANS, RED ONION, AND GRAPE TOMATO SALAD

What tastes great on arugula salad? Steak, of course! Kick it up with some white beans, red onion, and grape tomatoes, and you've got yourself one lean, mean steak salad. Serve this in the summer when the grill is hot, along with some of Lana's Famous Grilled Corn on the Cob (page 137), and you will have one hell of a barbecue.

7 tablespoons extra virgin olive oil, divided

2 red onions, sliced

2 cloves garlic, minced

Salt and pepper, to taste

8–10 shiitake mushrooms with stems, cut into ½-inch-thick slices

1 (15-ounce) can cannellini beans, juice drained and rinsed

3 pounds thick-cut flank steak

½ pound baby arugula

3 tablespoons red wine vinegar

In a frying pan, heat 3 tablespoons olive oil over medium-high heat. Add onion, garlic, salt, and pepper, and reduce the heat to medium. Cook, stirring, until onion is tender, about 10 minutes. Add the shiitake mushrooms and continue to cook, stirring until the mushrooms become wilted and soft, another 5 minutes. Add the beans and cook for 2 minutes more. Remove from heat, place the mixture into a bowl, and set aside to cool to room temperature.

Wash the frying pan and heat the pan on high, adding salt to the pan. Once hot, place the flank steak in the pan and cook for 6 minutes on each side for medium-rare; add 3 minutes per side for well-done. Once the meat is cooked, place the meat on a cutting board and let sit for 5 to 6 minutes. Slice the steak into whatever thickness you prefer.

In a large salad bowl, combine arugula with remaining 4 tablespoons olive oil and red wine vinegar. Add bean mixture and toss well. Arrange slices of steak on individual plates, and top with salad.

SERVES 4 TO 6

STEAK SICILIAN OREGANATA

Now here's a family favorite that goes over well for dinner and then for lunch the following day. Who would have ever thought a plain piece of meat like London broil could taste so incredibly good? If we have leftovers, we make sure to put it on fresh Italian bread for the kids to have for lunch the next day.

2½ pounds London broil

½ cup olive oil

1 cup seasoned bread crumbs

¼ cup grated Pecorino-Romano cheese

½ tablespoon fresh basil

2–3 cloves garlic, minced

Salt and pepper, to taste

½ lemon

Preheat oven to 400F.

Coat the London broil on all sides with the olive oil, and let sit for at least 30 minutes. On a shallow platter, combine bread crumbs, grated cheese, basil, garlic, salt, and pepper. Dip the meat in the bread crumb mixture and coat all sides. Place the meat on a baking sheet and squeeze the lemon on top of the meat. Bake for 8 to 10 minutes for medium, and 12 to 15 minutes for medium-well to well-done.

SERVES 4 TO 6

TRIPE ALLA ROMANA

A Wing and a Clam was the perfect restaurant for the "land lover" and the "sea lover." Dad had a great menu of both meats and fish, and always spent time in the kitchen himself among the chefs. This was his "hangout." All of Dad's pals came to the restaurant as well, including our cousin, the famous fighter Rocky Graziano, to shoot the breeze and savor Dad's Wednesday special: Tripe alla Romana. Dad and Rocky would always talk boxing and they would tell us stories about how Dad was a "street boxer" with a knockout punch better than some guys in the ring.

6 pounds tripe, well cleaned

½ cup olive oil

6 cloves garlic, chopped

1 large onion, chopped

Salt and pepper, to taste

1 pinch crushed red pepper flakes

2 (28-ounce) cans crushed San Marzano plum tomatoes

2 tablespoons fresh parsley, minced

3 potatoes, each cut into 6 or 8 pieces (optional)

Make sure the tripe is thoroughly cleaned by rinsing under cold water until all the grit is gone. Fill a 3-quart pot with cold water and bring to a boil. Add the tripe and boil for 10 minutes, then reduce heat to medium and cook the tripe for 1½ hours more. Rinse twice under cold water, and cut the tripe into finger-sized pieces.

Heat olive oil in a saucepan over medium heat, then add garlic, onion, salt, pepper, and red pepper flakes. Increase the heat to medium-high and add the tripe; brown the tripe for 5 to 6 minutes. Add the tomatoes and parsley. Increase heat and boil sauce for 5 minutes, then reduce heat and simmer for 1½ hours. If using potatoes, add them to the sauce after it has been cooking for 40 minutes.

SERVES 4

STEAK PIZZAIOLA

Jennifer's son, Justin, could never quite understand this dish. When he was two or three years old, he thought it was steak on top of pizza. We always tried to tell him that it was more like pizza on top of steak! Now that he's older, he understands exactly what this dish and, even more so, how delicious it is.

1 pound extra-wide noodles

2 rib-eye steaks, cut into 1½-inch pieces

Salt and pepper, to taste

½ teaspoon onion powder

¼ teaspoon garlic powder

3 tablespoons olive oil

2–3 cloves garlic, minced

1 sweet onion, sliced

1 (28-ounce) can crushed San Marzano tomatoes

10 whole white mushrooms, quartered

¼ cup red wine

3–4 fresh basil leaves, each torn into 2 or 3 pieces

Bring a pot of water to a boil and cook noodles according to package instructions. Drain and rinse noodles under cold water and set aside. Season the meat with salt, pepper, onion powder, and garlic powder. Heat olive oil in a large sauté pan over medium heat. Add garlic and onion and cook for 3 or 4 minutes, until the onions are translucent. Add the meat, cooking on each side for about 2 minutes. Transfer meat to a plate, and set aside. Add tomatoes, mushrooms, wine, and basil. Boil mixture for 2 minutes, then reduce heat and simmer for 15 to 20 minutes. Add meat to pan and cook for 10 additional minutes. Serve over noodles.

SERVES 4 TO 6

BEEF STEW

Now, if there is any dish in this book that reminds us of our mom, it has to be this one. Beef stew was her father, Anthony Gebbia's, favorite and she made it for him each and every time he came over. We also ate it at least once a week during the winter. (So much so that it became a running joke in the family and every time someone came over they would say, "What's for dinner . . . beef stew?") We can remember as far back as the '70s, when Mom used to use the Crock-Pot or the pressure cooker to make this dish . . . and still does. One would think she would have evolved by now, but Ronnie likes to keep it old school—and we don't complain because her dish is really delicious. This is fantastic served with a big loaf of crusty Italian bread.

3 tablespoons olive oil

1 large sweet onion, chopped

2 cloves garlic, chopped

2 pounds boneless beef chuck, cut into 2-inch pieces

1 (15-ounce) can San Marzano tomato sauce

1 (14.5-ounce) can beef stock

½ cup water

4–5 carrots, cut into bite-size pieces

3 red bliss potatoes, each cut into 8 pieces

Heat olive oil in a saucepan over medium-high heat, and sauté onion and garlic for 5 to 6 minutes. Add meat and brown on all sides, 3 or 4 minutes. Add the tomatoes and cook for 15 minutes. Add beef stock and water. Increase heat to high and cook until mixture boils. Add carrots and potatoes, and boil for another 5 minutes. Reduce heat and let simmer for 1 hour. Meat should be very tender; if not, cook for an additional 20 to 30 minutes.

SERVES 4

OUR TRADITIONAL MEAT LOAF

This is Mom's favorite dish to cook. Lord forgive Renee, but she couldn't stand eating meat loaf. She sneaked it to the dog, but Mom always offered her more. Renee would rather eat Brussels sprouts than meat loaf, but Jennifer and Lana loved it. This recipe is scrumptious, especially when served with Ricotta Cheese Mashed Potatoes (page 129).

6 fresh plum tomatoes

3 tablespoons olive oil

Salt and pepper, to taste

3 large cloves garlic, minced

1 pound ground beef

1 pound ground veal

1 pound ground pork

3 large eggs

½ cup seasoned bread crumbs

1 small sweet onion, diced

⅓ cup grated Pecorino-Romano cheese

¼ cup finely chopped fresh parsley

2 tablespoons finely chopped fresh basil

In a small bowl, combine the tomatoes, olive oil, salt, pepper, and one-quarter of the garlic. Set aside.

Preheat oven to 375F.

In a large bowl, combine ground beef, ground veal, and ground pork. Add eggs, bread crumbs, onion, grated cheese, remaining garlic, parsley, basil, salt, and pepper. Using your hands, mix all the ingredients together and shape mixture into a loaf. Place in a 9 × 13-inch baking pan and, with two fingers, press down the whole loaf about 1 inch and pour the tomato salad on top. Bake for 1 hour to 1 hour and 15 minutes. Let meat loaf rest for 8 to 10 minutes before slicing.

SERVES 4 TO 6

BEEF POT ROAST
WITH POTATOES AND CARROTS

This doesn't sound too Italian, does it? Well, Dad didn't care. When he was "away" in Minnesota, we used to visit him quite often. The whole family would jump on a plane and go to visit the Twin Cities. We would spend a day in the amazing, larger-than-life mall and explore the city. Then we would make a trek to the local supermarket, buying up everything Dad loved. Dad was in a low-security camp and was able to walk the grounds free, and the inmates were on the honor system to return. Well, Dad always returned from his walks, but usually with a box full of food he just happened to "find" in the woods. We laugh at the stories he told us about trying to sneak the food back into the prison, especially since Mom always bought the wrong things—like pot roast. He asked for small cans and jars and mostly fresh vegetables—tomatoes, onion, garlic, parsley— so he and his friends could make fresh sauce inside. But one time Mom brought him one of his favorite winter meals—beef pot roast with potatoes and carrots. He said it was hell hiding a roast in his uniform and he ultimately was caught with a slab of meat in his pants!

1 (4–5-pound) chuck beef roast

Salt and pepper, to taste

3 tablespoons olive oil

2 onions, peeled and quartered

8 whole carrots, unpeeled and cut in half

4 red bliss potatoes, each cut into 8 pieces

2 sprigs fresh rosemary

1 cup red wine (optional)

3 cups beef stock

Preheat oven to 325F.

Sprinkle roast with salt and pepper. In a large baking pan, add the olive oil and place the vegetables around the meat. Place the rosemary on top of the meat and add the wine, if using, and beef stock to the bottom of the pan. Bake in the oven for 1½ hours. Check to make sure the meat is cooked all the way through by cutting into the roast; it should be just a little pink. If it's not cooked through, bake for another 20 minutes.

SERVES 4 TO 6

PRIME RIB ROAST

Mom makes this dish the best. Us girls are meat and fish lovers at heart, and a good prime rib cooked medium-rare and sliced thick was a favorite on Easter Sunday (especially for Jennifer, who doesn't eat the traditional ham). Serve this with a batch of creamy mashed potatoes and smother them both with au jus, and you're in a meat lover's heaven.

3 tablespoons olive oil

Salt and pepper, to taste

4 cloves garlic, minced

1 tablespoon minced fresh parsley

1 tablespoon fresh basil

1 tablespoon fresh rosemary

1 (6-pound) bone-in rib roast

2 tablespoons salted butter, softened

Preheat oven to 400F.

In a bowl, combine oil, salt, pepper, garlic, parsley, basil, and rosemary. Rub mixture on top of the roast, and place the butter on top. Place the roast, fat side up, in a 9 × 13-inch baking pan. Cook the meat 10 to 12 minutes per pound for medium-rare. If you like it on the rare side, cook for 8 to 10 minutes per pound. Roast for 12 to 14 minutes per pound for well-done. When the roast is finished, take the pan out of the oven and let meat sit for 10 minutes before slicing. Save the juices from the pan and pour over mashed potatoes.

SERVES 4 TO 6

BRAISED SHORT RIBS

This is one of our all-time favorites in this cookbook. All three of us love this dish. Come on, wouldn't you, too? The ribs are slow-cooked to perfection with a sauce so delicious it's almost too good to be true. The way the meat falls off the bone and melts in your mouth is just incredible. It's like culinary heaven.

4 tablespoons olive oil, divided

5 pounds beef short ribs (8–12 ribs)

Salt and pepper, to taste

½ cup chopped carrots (cut in ½-inch circles)

1 onion, diced

4–5 cloves garlic, diced

1 teaspoon paprika

1 teaspoon ground coriander

¾ (28-ounce) can crushed San Marzano tomatoes

2 tablespoons chopped fresh parsley

1½ cups dry red wine

1½ cups water

½ cup beef stock

Preheat oven to 350F.

In an 8-quart Dutch oven pan, heat 2 tablespoons oil over medium heat. Season the ribs with salt and pepper and brown them on each side, about 4 minutes per side. If all the ribs won't fit at one time, brown them in two batches. Drain off the fat. Transfer ribs to a plate and set aside.

In the same pan, add the remaining 2 tablespoons olive oil, carrots, onion, garlic, salt, and pepper. Cook over medium heat, stirring and scraping up any browned bits from the bottom of the pan, until the vegetables are soft and lightly browned, 6 to 8 minutes. Add paprika, coriander, tomatoes, and parsley, and stir well to combine. Add the wine, increase heat to high, and cook for 2 to 3 minutes, until mixture reduces. Return ribs and any juices that have collected on the plate to the pan along with water and beef stock. Increase heat to high and boil sauce for 2 minutes, and then reduce to a simmer and cook for about 3 hours, turning ribs occasionally, until meat is falling off the bones.

SERVES 4 TO 6

Lana's and Renee's kids—
Anthony, John, AJ, and Sonni

Jennifer as a baby

Veronica, Jennifer, and Renee
with Li'l John, Lana's son

4

POULTRY

NO CHICKENS ALLOWED

You gotta be a tough guy to hang around with us girls and be in the mob. You can't be scared, and you can't let them see you sweat. In other words, no chickens allowed. This ain't the mob, however, and we ain't talking about the streets. We're talking about food so we're making an exception here and giving you the best chicken recipes in town—Chicken Marsala, Chicken Cutlet Parmesan, Chicken Scarpariello, and Chicken Cutlet Milanese with Goat Cheese Salad. Each one is better than the next!

CHICKEN CACCIATORE

This is a traditional Italian chicken dish made to perfection by Grandma and enjoyed by all. Grandma would never let us order this dish when we were out, claiming that the restaurants commercialized all of our Italian foods. She got so angry when she saw these dishes on the menu, and very rarely did we take her out to eat Italian. She couldn't stand eating what she believed she could make better at home.

½ cup flour, for dredging

1 whole fryer chicken, cut up

¼ cup olive oil

1 onion, diced

5 cloves garlic, chopped

Salt and pepper, to taste

¼ cup dry wine

1 (28-ounce) can Italian crushed tomatoes

8–10 leaves fresh basil

1 pound white mushrooms, cut in half

1 cup black olives, pitted

Put the flour into a medium-sized bowl and dredge the chicken pieces to coat. In a large sauté pan, heat olive oil over medium-high heat. Add the chicken and sauté until brown, about 5 minutes per side. If all of the chicken doesn't fit into the pan, cook it in two batches. Transfer the chicken to a plate and set aside.

Add onion and garlic to the same pan and sauté over medium heat until tender, about 5 minutes. Season with salt and pepper, to taste. Add wine and simmer to reduce liquid by half, about 8 minutes. Add tomatoes and basil, increase heat to high, and bring to a boil. Boil for 5 minutes, and then reduce heat to medium-low. Add the chicken to the mixture along with the mushrooms and olives. Turn every 10 minutes for another 35 to 40 minutes, until done.

SERVES 4 TO 6

CHICKEN MARSALA

There are a bunch of traditional Italian dishes you will find at most Italian restaurants, and chicken Marsala is one of them. Italians love wine, and they love nothing more than to cook with it. This perfect blend of Marsala wine and mushrooms leaves your palate and especially your stomach fully satisfied.

4 boneless, skinless chicken breast halves

¼ cup all-purpose flour

½ teaspoon salt

¼ teaspoon pepper

½ teaspoon dried basil

3 tablespoons olive oil

3 tablespoons butter

¾ cup fresh mushrooms, sliced

½ cup Marsala wine

Place the chicken between sheets of plastic wrap and pound with a mallet to ¼-inch thickness. In a bowl mix the flour, salt, pepper, and basil. Heat the oil and butter in a large sauté pan over medium-high heat. Dredge the chicken in the seasoned flour mixture. Cook chicken until lightly browned on one side, 2 to 3 minutes. Turn chicken and add mushrooms around the chicken pieces. Cook about 2 minutes longer, until lightly browned, stirring the mushrooms. Add Marsala wine to pan. Reduce heat to medium-low, cover, and simmer for 10 minutes.

SERVES 4

CHICKEN SCARPARIELLO

Cooking this meal was probably the most time we spent in the kitchen together at one time. It was a real team effort that the entire family needed to be in on. It wasn't because it is such a hard dish to make, but because everyone wanted to make sure she received her fair share to eat. We definitely love this chicken dish a little more than the others. Everyone had her own jobs for this dish, but the result is absolutely delicious.

½ cup olive oil

2 (½-pound) chickens, rinsed, patted dry, spines removed, each cut into 12 pieces

4 links Italian sausage (2 hot and 2 sweet), cut into 1-inch pieces

1 large red bell pepper, seeded and cut into thin strips

1 large sweet onion, sliced

4–5 cloves garlic

3–4 hot cherry peppers, left whole (optional, if you like a little kick)

2–3 small potatoes, boiled and sliced (optional)

½ cup chicken broth

¼ cup dry white wine

¼ cup red wine vinegar

1 tablespoon fresh parsley, chopped

Salt and pepper, to taste

Heat olive oil in a large sauté pan over medium-high heat. Brown the chicken in batches, about 5 minutes per side. Remove the chicken and drain on paper towels. Add the sausage to the pan and sauté until brown. Use a ladle to skim out about half the oil, leaving sausage in the pan. Add bell peppers, onion, and garlic and sauté until soft and beginning to brown, about 10 minutes.

Return chicken to pan. Add cherry peppers, potatoes, if using, chicken broth, wine, vinegar, parsley, salt, and pepper. Cover and simmer until chicken is cooked through, about 12 minutes. Uncover and continue cooking until the sauce has reduced slightly, about 15 minutes.

SERVES 4

LANA'S CHICKEN SOUP

Whenever any of us would get sick, Lana would whip up her famous spicy chicken soup, which she adapted from Grandma's recipe. This soup could cure anything, and within hours we were always feeling better. It could be made spicy or not spicy, or you can make it Granny-style with some added Italian ingredients.

1 large whole soup chicken

1 head escarole

3 tablespoons olive oil

2 cloves garlic, diced

2 onions, diced

1–2 habañero peppers, sliced, depending on your preferred level of heat

6 plum tomatoes, diced

3 cups chicken stock

2 cups cold water

3 celery stalks

6 carrots, chopped into chunks

Salt and pepper, to taste

1 pound cooked ditalini pasta (or any small pasta or rice)

Soak the chicken in cold, salted water to clean.

Prepare the escarole: Remove any damaged outside leaves, and wash thoroughly under cold water. Cut the escarole in half, and cut each half in half and then cut across again. Set aside.

In a 4-quart saucepan, heat olive oil over medium heat and sauté garlic, onions, habañero, and tomatoes for 6 to 8 minutes. Remove chicken from water, place in the pot with the sautéed ingredients, and cook over medium-high heat, until brown on all sides. After the chicken is browned, add the chicken stock and water, making sure there is enough liquid to cover the top of the chicken. Bring to a boil and cook for 10 to 15 minutes, stirring frequently. Reduce heat to medium-low. Add celery, carrots, escarole, salt, and pepper.

Cook for about 1½ hours until chicken is falling off the bone. Carefully remove chicken and let cool. Remove all the meat from the bone, cut into bite-size pieces, and add to the soup. Cook for another 30 minutes.

We love this soup with a little ditalini pasta. Place a small scoop of pasta and 2 scoops of soup in each bowl.

SERVES 6 TO 8

CHICKEN CUTLET PARMESAN

You can't get more old school than a good, old-fashioned chicken Parm. This dish is found in pizzerias and just about every Italian establishment in the world, so we had to include it in our book. And, of course, anything with chicken cutlets is one of Jennifer's all-time favorites. Chicken cutlet, pan-fried to perfection, with zesty marinara sauce on top and finished with some good old fresh mozzarella melted to gooey perfection—delicious! You can also make this dish with veal cutlets if you prefer.

8 chicken cutlets

3–4 tablespoons olive oil

2–3 cloves garlic, minced

1 onion, diced

1 (28-ounce) can crushed San Marzano tomatoes

3–4 fresh basil leaves, torn

Salt and pepper, to taste

2 eggs

1 tablespoon milk

2 cups seasoned bread crumbs

2 tablespoons finely chopped fresh parsley

¾ cup grated Pecorino-Romano cheese

1 cup vegetable oil

8 (½-inch-thick) slices mozzarella cheese

Place the chicken cutlets between pieces of wax paper and pound with a kitchen mallet to ¼-inch thickness. Heat olive oil in a sauté pan over medium heat. Add garlic and onion and sauté until onions are translucent. Add tomatoes, basil, salt, and pepper, to taste. Boil for 2 to 3 minutes, then reduce heat and simmer for 40 minutes.

Preheat oven to 350F.

In a bowl, beat the eggs, milk, salt, and pepper, to taste. In another bowl, combine bread crumbs, parsley, and grated cheese. Dip each piece of chicken in egg wash, then in the bread crumb mixture; coat well.

In a frying pan, heat vegetable oil over medium-high heat. Add the breaded chicken cutlets and cook, turning once, until golden brown, about 2 minutes per side. Transfer chicken to a baking sheet. Top each cutlet with sauce and a slice of mozzarella. Bake for 10 to 12 minutes until mozzarella starts to bubble.

SERVES 6

CHICKEN PICCATA

Capers are Renee's favorite. As a kid, she would mix them with tuna fish and eat it on top of Doritos! She was always the eccentric one, both in and out of the kitchen. That Renee! As she got older, however, this (and Veal Piccata) became her favorite to both cook and eat. If you ask Renee, capers should be put on everything!

6–8 chicken cutlets

½ cup flour

Salt and pepper, to taste

3–4 tablespoons vegetable oil

1 tablespoon olive oil

1 tablespoon salted butter

2 cloves garlic, chopped

¼ cup dry white wine

½ cup chicken stock

Juice of 1 lemon

1 teaspoon honey

2 tablespoons salted capers, rinsed

1 tablespoon finely chopped fresh parsley

Place the chicken cutlets between pieces of wax paper and pound with a kitchen mallet to ¼-inch thickness. In a bowl, mix together flour, salt, and pepper. Dredge the cutlets in the flour, coating thoroughly. In a frying pan, heat the vegetable oil over medium heat and slightly brown each piece of chicken, about 2 minutes on each side. Set aside.

In a large sauté pan, heat olive oil and butter over medium heat. Add the garlic and gently stir until tender, about 2 minutes. Add the wine to the pan and increase heat to high for 1 minute, then reduce heat and simmer to deglaze the wine, about 3 minutes. Slowly add chicken stock, lemon juice, honey, and capers and simmer until the liquid has reduced by half, 3 to 4 minutes. Stir in the parsley and add the chicken cutlets back to the pan. Simmer for 3 minutes on each side, until nicely browned. Serve over mashed potatoes or rice.

SERVES 4

CHICKEN WITH SAUSAGE, PEPPERS, AND ONIONS

This is a variation of the San Gennaro feast specialty, but with chicken added. The feast was a must-do in the Graziano household. We believe this is where Renee first got her fever for fame. We were like mini celebrities there. Everyone knew us and knew Dad. As we walked down the street, we were always stopped by one or another of Dad's "friends" and invited to sit and eat. Often it was this dish but instead of pairing it with soda, we just had to have it with a Shirley Temple on the side. Don't forget to enjoy this, hero-style, on a nice piece of Italian bread!

3 bone-in chicken breast halves

Salt and pepper, to taste

3 tablespoons olive oil, divided

4 links Italian sweet sausage (or 2 sweet links and 2 hot links)

2 onions, sliced ¼-inch thick

1 large red bell pepper, cut into ¼-inch strips

3 whole hot cherry peppers, seeds removed and cut into ¼-inch strips

3 cloves garlic, minced

2 teaspoons sugar

⅓ cup white wine vinegar

¾ cup plus 1 tablespoon chicken stock

1 teaspoon cornstarch

1 tablespoon fresh parsley, minced

Preheat oven to 350F. Season the chicken on both sides with salt and pepper. Set aside.

Heat 1 teaspoon oil in a frying pan set over medium-high heat. Add the sausage and cook, stirring to break the sausage into ½-inch pieces, until browned, about 3 minutes. Place the sausage on a plate lined with paper towels. Remove the frying pan from the heat and pour the fat into a small bowl and reserve. Wipe out the pan with paper towels.

Return the frying pan to the stove on medium-high heat and heat the rest of the oil until smoking. Now add the chicken, skin side down, and cook 3 to 4 minutes per side, until chicken is brown. Remove the chicken and place on a plate. Pour the fat from the pan into the bowl with the sausage fat, and wipe the pan out with paper towels. Return the frying pan to medium-high heat and heat 1 tablespoon reserved fat until simmering. Add the onion and cook until it begins to soften, about 2 minutes. Add the peppers and cherry peppers and cook, stirring occasionally, until the peppers begin to soften, about 5 minutes. Add garlic and cook, stirring frequently. Add sugar, vinegar, and ¾ cup chicken stock, and bring mixture to a boil, scraping up browned bits from bottom of pan.

(RECIPE CONTINUES)

Add everything from the frying pan into a 9 × 13-inch baking pan. Place the sausage and the chicken on top, skin side up, and any chicken juices that have collected on the plate. Bake for 25 to 35 minutes, until chicken is no longer pink; bake another 10 minutes, if necessary. While the sausage and chicken is baking, mix the cornstarch in a bowl with remaining 1 tablespoon chicken stock.

When the chicken is finished, take everything out of the baking dish and place it on a platter. Take the juices and scraps from the baking pan and add back into the frying pan, then add the parsley. Simmer for 2 or 3 minutes, then add the cornstarch mixture. Cook for another 3 minutes, until the sauce thickens, then pour over chicken and serve.

SERVES 4 TO 6

CHICKEN ROLLS WITH FONTINA CHEESE

Anything with cheese is absolutely delicious, and the Grazianos certainly love their cheese. Get ready for a culinary explosion because Fontina adds just the right amount of flavor to ordinary chicken. This dish is delicious over rice.

6 chicken cutlets

Salt and pepper, to taste

6 sage leaves

¾ cup grated Fontina cheese

3 tablespoons olive oil

3 cloves garlic, halved

⅓ cup white wine

1 (28-ounce) can whole San Marzano tomatoes

Pinch crushed red pepper flakes

Place chicken cutlets between pieces of wax paper and pound with a kitchen mallet until about ¼-inch thin. Place the cutlets on a plate and sprinkle with salt and pepper. Place one sage leaf crosswise on each piece of chicken, and sprinkle each piece with Fontina cheese. Roll up the chicken and seal with two toothpicks, one on each end.

In a frying pan, heat the olive oil over medium-high heat and sauté garlic until slightly browned, 2 to 3 minutes. Add the chicken rolls and brown them on all sides, 2 to 3 minutes per side. Remove the chicken from pan, and discard garlic. Set chicken aside. Add wine and simmer for 2 minutes, scraping up browned bits from the bottom of the pan with a wooden spoon.

Crush the tomatoes a bit with your hands. In a blender, combine tomatoes, salt, pepper, and red pepper flakes, and blend until smooth. Add the tomato mixture to pan. Simmer for 5 or 6 minutes, to allow flavors to mix.

Return the chicken to the pan and simmer for 10 to 12 minutes. Turn the chicken over and simmer until cooked through, 5 to 7 minutes more. Remove the chicken from the pan and remove the toothpicks. Place the chicken on a platter; pour tomato sauce over each piece.

SERVES 4

CRISPY BAKED CHICKEN WITH HERBS

Baked—yes. Crispy—yes. Herbs—oh yeah! Want to know how to make a dish that sounds this great? Ask our mom. This was one of our family's staples on an ordinary dinner night. Mom always cooked the chicken to perfection so it was a golden brown on the outside, but with crispy skin and juicy insides. This is great served with Roasted Potatoes (page 136).

⅓ cup instant potato flakes

¼ cup grated Pecorino-Romano cheese

2 tablespoons fresh parsley

Salt and pepper, to taste

½ teaspoon onion powder

¼ teaspoon garlic powder

¼ cup (½ stick) salted butter

1 (3½-pound) fryer chicken, cut up (about 18 pieces)

Preheat oven to 375F.

In a bowl, combine potato flakes, grated cheese, parsley, salt, pepper, onion powder, and garlic powder. Mix well. Microwave butter for 20 seconds to soften, and place it on a flat plate. Dip the chicken pieces in the butter, and then in the potato flake mixture, coating thoroughly. Place the chicken in a baking pan and bake for 45 to 50 minutes, until golden brown.

SERVES 4 TO 6

CHICKEN ROLLATINI

Chicken rollatini is so delicious and easy to make. We recommend you make this for your kids. Ours sure do love it! This is perfect served with some ditalini pasta and butter.

6 chicken cutlets

2 tablespoons olive oil

2–3 cloves garlic, minced

3 cups chopped baby spinach leaves

1 egg

1 tablespoon milk

Salt and pepper, to taste

1 cup seasoned bread crumbs

⅓ cup grated Pecorino-Romano cheese

4 slices prosciutto, cut in half

4 slices provolone cheese, cut in half

¼ cup vegetable oil

3 tablespoons salted butter

Preheat oven to 400F.

Place the chicken cutlets between sheets of plastic wrap and pound with a kitchen mallet to ¼-inch thickness. In a frying pan, heat the olive oil over medium heat. Add garlic and sauté until slightly browned, then add the spinach. Cook until spinach is wilted, 6 to 8 minutes. Add butter to spinach and mix until melted. Drain liquid from the pan, and set spinach aside.

In a bowl, whisk egg and milk with salt and pepper. In another bowl, combine bread crumbs and grated cheese. Place each chicken cutlet on a flat surface and top with a piece of prosciutto and a piece of provolone. Spread 1½ tablespoons spinach mixture over each piece of cheese, then roll up the cutlet and tie in 3 spots with kitchen twine to secure. Dip each roll in the egg wash, and then in the bread crumbs, coating thoroughly.

In a frying pan, heat the vegetable oil over medium heat, and brown rolls on all sides. Transfer the chicken to a baking pan and bake for 20 minutes, until chicken is cooked through.

SERVES 4 TO 6

ROASTED WHOLE CHICKEN WITH VEGETABLES

If you're looking for a one-pot dinner, this has got to be one of the best and easiest to make. All of the ingredients are combined and then cooked in one baking dish. Our mom made this dish the best, but it always came out fine among us sisters. Jenn likes the legs and thighs, Renee likes the wings, and Lana loves the breasts . . . so this is one dish we never had to fight over!

1 (3–4-pound) oven-roaster chicken

3 oranges, halved

1 lemon, halved

2 sprigs fresh oregano

2 tablespoons fresh parsley

2 sprigs fresh rosemary

2 tablespoons olive oil, divided

2 tablespoons salted butter

Salt and pepper, to taste

1 teaspoon onion powder

½ teaspoon garlic powder

4–5 carrots, cut into 1-inch circles

2 sweet onions

6 red bliss potatoes, each cut into 8 pieces

4 cloves garlic

⅓ cup chicken stock

Preheat oven to 375F.

Remove everything from the inside of the chicken and discard. Rinse chicken under cold water and salt the outside and cavity. Stuff the cavity with the oranges, lemons, oregano, parsley, and rosemary. Tie the ends of the drumsticks together with kitchen string.

Rub the chicken all over with 1 tablespoon oil and the butter, and sprinkle with salt, pepper, onion, and garlic powder. Place the chicken, vegetables, garlic, and chicken stock in a 9 × 13-inch roasting pan and drizzle the remaining 1 tablespoon oil over the chicken. Roast for 50 to 60 minutes, turning vegetables once, until golden brown.

SERVES 4 TO 6

CHICKEN CUTLET MILANESE WITH GOAT CHEESE SALAD

This dish is made with Jennifer's all-time favorite food on Earth—chicken cutlets. This was passed down from Grandma Nora to Mom, and then to Jenn. She makes them the best out of all of us, and that's probably because she has taste-tested so many of them! We always joke that Jennifer is the favorite child so each and every time she returned home from college, we always knew what Mom was going to make for dinner. We used to tease Mom and have pounds of chicken cutlets delivered to her house whenever we knew Jennifer was coming home. Lo and behold, Mom would cook up her favorite dish for her favorite daughter. And trust us, we weren't allowed to touch one cutlet until Jennifer arrived and all of the leftovers were saved for her to bring back to NYU. Mom loved us all, but if there was any indication of special treatment, it was through chicken cutlets for Jennifer.

6 chicken cutlets

1 cup romaine lettuce, chopped into bite-size pieces

1 cup arugula

8 grape tomatoes

2 cups spinach

½ cup goat cheese

Juice of 2 lemons

⅓ cup olive oil

Salt and pepper, to taste

2 eggs

1 tablespoon milk

1 cup seasoned bread crumbs

⅓ cut grated Pecorino-Romano cheese

⅓ cup vegetable oil

Place the chicken cutlets between sheets of plastic wrap and pound with a kitchen mallet to ¼-inch thickness. Set aside.

Make the salad: In a large bowl, mix the romaine, arugula, tomatoes, spinach, and goat cheese. In a small bowl, whisk the lemon juice, olive oil, and a pinch of salt and pepper. Set aside. Don't toss the dressing with the salad until you're ready to serve, so that it doesn't become soggy.

In a bowl, whisk the eggs and milk with another pinch of salt and pepper. In another bowl, mix the bread crumbs and grated cheese. Dip each cutlet in the egg wash and then in the bread crumbs, coating each thoroughly. In a frying pan, heat the vegetable oil over medium-high heat and fry each cutlet until golden brown, 4 to 5 minutes on each side. Place cutlets on paper towels to absorb the excess oil.

Place the cutlets on a serving platter. Combine salad and dressing, and evenly divide among cutlets to serve.

SERVES 4 TO 6

Jennifer and Renee

Veronica Graziano and her grandsons AJ and Justin

VEAL AND LAMB

ALWAYS A "HIT"

You may not know it but veal—aka the meat of young calves—is a very big deal to Italians. Veal has been an important ingredient in Italian cuisine since ancient times. Italians love it and, although it isn't always fully represented at all restaurants, it's a type of meat Italians eat a lot at home. Additionally, lamb is important to Italians and traditionally eaten in the spring around Easter time. Try Veal Piccata, Veal Cutlet Parmesan, Veal Osso Buco, or Veal Chop Pizzaiola, or try Roasted Leg of Lamb with Rosemary and Garlic or Lamb Stew with Dumplings—we guarantee your guests will love these and you will be a hit (not the subject of one!).

ROASTED LEG OF LAMB WITH ROSEMARY AND GARLIC

Leg of lamb has always reminded us of Easter dinner as lamb is typically associated with the holiday. But nobody loves leg of lamb like Ricotta Finotta! Who is that, you ask? Well, that is our old Italian aunt straight from Italy—except she doesn't exist. It is actually Renee's alter ego. Every year on Easter, Renee stuffs my grandmother's old dresses with pillows, dons a gray wig, glues a thick black hair to her chin. and transforms into Ricotta Finotta. All day all the nieces and nephews have to call her "Ricotta Finotta" or she just won't answer. Renee has many personalities, but Ricotta Finotta is our favorite.

1 (6½-pound) leg of lamb, trimmed of excess fat

Salt and pepper, to taste

2 tablespoons olive oil

2 tablespoons fresh rosemary, minced

1 tablespoon lemon peel, finely grated

3–4 cloves garlic, minced

¼ cup water

Preheat oven to 350F.

In a baking pan, place the lamb fat side up. Sprinkle with salt and pepper. Mix the oil, rosemary, lemon peel, and garlic together in a bowl. Rub the mixture all over the lamb.

Roast the lamb for an hour if you like it medium-rare. Halfway through, baste the lamb with the juices from the bottom of the baking pan. If you want the lamb to be medium, then cook it for another 15 minutes. When finished, transfer the lamb to a platter. Tent loosely with foil; let stand for 15 minutes.

Spoon off the fat from the drippings in the roasting pan; add ¼ cup water to the pan. Place on the burner over medium heat. Add any lamb juices from platter. Bring to a boil, scraping up browned bits on the bottom of the pan. Cut the lamb into thin slices; arrange on the platter. Pour pan juices over top.

SERVES 6 TO 8

VEAL CHOP MILANESE WITH ARUGULA SALAD

This is another one of Jennifer's favorites. A good veal chop pounded thin and smothered with salad . . . it's the very best. The colors alone in this dish are beautiful enough to whet the palate—stunning reds and greens on top of veal fried just right. Jennifer likes to add some fresh mozzarella chunks and extra balsamic glaze to her salad, but you can eat it any way you'd like— it's always delicious.

4 bone-in veal chops (12 ounces each)

2 cups flour

4 large eggs

2 cups seasoned bread crumbs

Salt and pepper, to taste

¾ cup grated Parmigiano-Reggiano cheese

¼ cup olive oil

2 tablespoons salted butter

2 cloves garlic, minced

Juice from ½ lemon

1 red onion, sliced

¼ cup extra virgin olive oil

3 cups fresh arugula

1 cup grape tomatoes, halved

8 fresh basil leaves

Place the veal chops on a cutting board and cover them with plastic wrap. With a meat mallet, pound the meat to ¼-inch thick. Have 3 separate bowls ready; put the flour in one, crack the eggs in another, and place the bread crumbs in the third. Lightly mix the eggs with salt and pepper. Mix the grated cheese in with the bread crumbs. Dredge the chops in flour and shake off the excess, then dip them in the egg, and finally in bread crumbs to coat. Heat olive oil and butter in a large sauté pan over medium heat. Add veal chops and cook until golden brown, 4 to 6 minutes per side. Place on a paper towel–lined plate to absorb excess oil.

In a large mixing bowl, combine garlic, lemon juice, and red onion. Whisk in olive oil. Add the arugula, tomatoes, and basil to the dressing and gently toss together. To serve, place a veal chop in the center of each plate and top with salad.

SERVES 4

VEAL CUTLET PARMESAN

There is a very famous Italian restaurant uptown in New York City called Rao's. Some say it takes years on the waiting list to get a reservation and you have to know somebody who knows somebody to get one. We have been going there for years with Dad and now that we've grown up, we go with our own friends and families. Each and every time we eat there, Jennifer orders the veal Parm. She says it's the best in the world (among other items on their menu, of course) and she cannot leave the place without eating it. If you want a good side dish with this, you can always eat it with a nice Italian salad—but hands down it goes best with some spaghetti.

3–4 tablespoons olive oil

2–3 cloves garlic, minced

1 onion, diced

1 (28-ounce) can crushed San Marzano tomatoes

3–4 fresh basil leaves, torn

Salt and pepper, to taste

2 eggs

1 tablespoon milk

Salt and pepper, to taste

2 cups seasoned bread crumbs

2 tablespoons finely chopped fresh parsley

¾ cup grated Pecorino-Romano cheese

8 veal cutlets, pounded

1 cup vegetable oil

8 (½-inch-thick) slices mozzarella cheese

Heat olive oil in a sauté pan over medium heat. Add olive oil, garlic, and onion and cook until the onions are translucent. Add tomatoes, basil, salt, and pepper. Bring to a boil for 2 to 3 minutes, then reduce heat and simmer for 40 minutes. In a bowl, beat the eggs and milk together and add salt and pepper to taste. In another bowl, combine the bread crumbs, parsley, and grated cheese. Dip each piece of veal in the egg wash, followed by the bread crumb mixture, taking care to thoroughly coat veal.

Preheat oven to 350F.

In a frying pan, heat vegetable oil over medium-high heat. Add cutlets and cook, turning once until golden brown, about 2 minutes per side. Transfer veal to a baking sheet. Top each cutlet with tomato sauce and a slice of mozzarella. Bake for 10 to 12 minutes, until mozzarella starts to bubble.

SERVES 4 TO 6

VEAL SPIEDINI

What could be more enjoyable than the finest ingredients rolled up with juicy, tender veal? Nothing, that's what. Renee's son, AJ, is no stranger to this meal and always goes in for plate number two. He claims the stuffing is "where it's at," and will spoon up whatever has fallen out.

8 veal cutlets, sliced thin

1 cup grated Pecorino-Romano cheese

¼ cup bread crumbs

½ cup finely chopped fresh parsley

Salt and pepper, to taste

2 eggs

1 tablespoon milk

4 tablespoons vegetable oil

8 slices mozzarella cheese

8 fresh basil leaves

8 lemon wedges

Place the veal cutlets between pieces of wax paper, and set them aside. In a mixing bowl, mix together the grated cheese, bread crumbs, parsley, and salt and pepper. In another bowl, beat together eggs and milk. Dip each piece of veal into egg wash and then into bread crumb mixture, making sure to thoroughly coat veal.

Heat vegetable oil in a frying pan set over medium heat, and cook veal until golden brown, 2 to 3 minutes per side. Transfer cutlets to a plate lined with paper towels, to absorb excess oil. Place a slice of mozzarella and a leaf of basil on each cutlet, roll up, and secure with toothpicks. Squeeze lemon over cutlets and serve at room temperature.

SERVES 4

VEAL PICCATA

Nothing can compare to the taste of veal sweetened with the ingredients of piccata. It's like a party you weren't invited to but crashed anyway. No one complains when this dish is served, especially Renee. Be sure to bust out our pinot grigio, which goes great with this dish.

8 veal cutlets

½ cup flour

Salt and pepper, to taste

⅓ cup vegetable oil

1 tablespoon olive oil

1 tablespoon salted butter

2 cloves garlic, chopped

¼ cup dry white wine

½ cup chicken stock

Juice from 1 lemon

2 tablespoons salted capers, rinsed

1 teaspoon honey

1 tablespoon finely chopped fresh parsley

Place the veal cutlets between pieces of wax paper and pound with a kitchen mallet to ¼-inch thickness. In a bowl, mix together flour, salt, and pepper. Dredge the cutlets in flour, taking care to thoroughly coat both sides. Heat vegetable oil in a frying pan set over medium heat, and slightly brown each piece of veal, about 2 minutes per side. Set aside.

In a large sauté pan, heat olive oil and butter over medium heat. Add the garlic and stir until tender, about 2 minutes. Increase heat to high, add wine to the pan, and boil for 1 minute, then reduce heat to a simmer to deglaze pan, 2 to 3 minutes. Add chicken stock, lemon juice, capers, and honey and simmer until the liquid has reduced by half, 3 or 4 minutes. Stir in the parsley, and add veal cutlets back to pan. Simmer for 3 minutes per side.

This is excellent served over mashed potatoes or rice.

SERVES 4 TO 6

LAMB STEW WITH DUMPLINGS

This is such a delicious dish on a cold winter's day. This recipe was passed down from Grandma to Mom to Lana, who has perfected it by adding the most delicious dumplings. Jennifer practices this dish often since it's one of her son, Justin's, favorites. She hasn't gotten it perfect just yet, however, and always calls Lana halfway through for advice. We hope you enjoy making this as much as we do—you'll definitely enjoy eating it.

3 tablespoons olive oil

2 large onions, chopped

2 lamb shanks

2 pounds lamb cubes

1 (14.5-ounce) can beef bouillon (or stock)

1 (15-ounce) can Goya tomato sauce

Salt and pepper, to taste

1 (20-ounce) box Bisquick

Heat olive oil in a 3-quart pot over medium-high heat. Add onion and sauté until translucent. Add lamb shank and lamb cubes and brown on all sides, about 5 minutes per side. Add beef stock, tomato sauce, and salt and pepper, to taste. Bring the sauce to a boil, making sure the meat is covered by the sauce. (If the sauce doesn't cover the meat, slowly add water until the meat is covered.) After it's boiled for at least 10 minutes, reduce heat to medium-low and simmer for 2 hours. Prepare and cook dumplings using package directions on the side of the Bisquick box. (You should have 10 to 12 dumplings for this size pot.)

SERVES 4 TO 6

VEAL SALTIMBOCCA

Got some basil growing in the garden? Good! Got some prosciutto sliced from your local Italian market? Good! Got some veal, too? Even better! Now, go make yourself some Graziano Saltimbocca and tell 'em Renee, Lana, and Jennifer made you do it. Make it a pasta, make it a main dish, or make it a made man—whatever you do, make sure to invite us over for dinner or pay the piper.

8 slices prosciutto

8 veal cutlets

1 cup flour

2 tablespoons olive oil

2 tablespoons salted butter

8 fresh basil leaves

½ cup dry white wine

¼ cup chicken stock

Salt and pepper, to taste

Place a slice of prosciutto on each veal cutlet, place cutlets between two sheets of wax paper, and pound with a kitchen mallet to ¼-inch thickness. Place flour in a bowl and dredge each piece of meat, coating thoroughly.

In a large sauté pan, heat the olive oil over medium-high heat. Cook the meat, prosciutto side down, turning once, until lightly browned on both sides, 2 to 3 minutes per side. Transfer to a plate and set aside.

Drain oil from pan, place the pan back over the heat, and add the butter. Add the basil and sauté for 1 minute. Add white wine and scrape loose any bits from bottom of pan, then add the chicken stock, salt, and pepper. Return cutlets back in pan, prosciutto side up, and cook until the sauce is reduced by half and the cutlets are heated through, about 5 minutes. Serve veal over mashed potatoes or rice.

SERVES 4 TO 6

VEAL OSSO BUCO

This is Dad's all-time favorite meat dish to order out! Nothing says "Leave me alone while I'm eating" like when you have a bowl of buco on the table. Our father actually came home an hour early just to wait at the table while Mom made this. Music tames the savage beast, right? Well, osso buco tames the irritable Italian—especially Dad. This goes very well with Asparagus Risotto (page 128).

4 veal shanks (about 1 pound each)

Salt and pepper, to taste

¼ cup vegetable oil

2 carrots, peeled and chopped

2 celery stalks, chopped

2 tablespoons fresh parsley

½ large onion, chopped

4 cloves garlic, chopped

1 cup dry white wine

4 fresh plum tomatoes, chopped

4 cups beef stock

1 bay leaf

Preheat oven to 350F.

Pat meat with paper towels to remove any moisture from veal shanks; this will make the meat brown easier. With a knife, make 4 cuts along the top of each shank, about 1 inch deep, so the meat won't twist out of shape. Season the shanks with salt and pepper.

In a cast-iron Dutch oven, heat oil over high heat, then add meat and sear it on both sides. When a brown crust has developed on all sides of the meat, remove from the pan and set aside. Reduce heat to medium, and add the carrots, celery, parsley, onion, and garlic and cook for 5 minutes, until the onion is slightly translucent. Add the wine and reduce liquid by half. Return the meat to the pot and add the tomatoes, stock, and bay leaf. The liquid should cover the veal shanks by three-quarters.

Increase heat to high, and boil liquid, 2 to 3 minutes. Cover and transfer to the oven. Cook for 2 hours, until the meat is tender.

SERVES 4

VEAL CHOP PIZZAIOLA

Jennifer's son, Justin, absolutely loves pizzaiola! He puts it on everything. There's something in that sauce that brings out a monster of flavor in the veal, and let us tell you: If you have any sauce left over, keep it. It makes a great condiment for burgers and sandwiches the next day.

2 cups white rice

4 veal chops, cut into 1½-inch pieces

Salt and pepper, to taste

½ teaspoon onion powder

¼ teaspoon garlic powder

3 tablespoons olive oil

2–3 cloves garlic, minced

1 sweet onion, sliced

1 (28-ounce) can crushed San Marzano tomatoes

10 whole white mushrooms, quartered

¼ cup red wine

3–4 fresh basil leaves, each torn into 2 or 3 pieces

Cook rice according to package instructions and set aside. Season the veal with salt, pepper, onion powder, and garlic powder. Heat olive oil in a large sauté pan over medium heat, and sauté garlic and onion for 3 or 4 minutes. Add veal chops, cooking 3 minutes per side. Remove chops from pan and set aside on a plate. Add tomatoes, mushrooms, wine, and basil to the pan and bring to a boil for 2 minutes, then reduce heat to a simmer for 15 to 20 minutes. Add the meat back to the pan and cook for another 10 minutes. Serve over the rice.

SERVES 4

VEAL CHOPS WITH MUSHROOMS AND CHERRY PEPPERS

This is another hearty dish that all the children can now make, though it is little John who has really mastered it. He knows exactly how long to cook that veal until it's sweet and tender enough to cut with a fork. Everyone wants to know when John is going to make this dish so that they can drop in unannounced. This is best served with roasted potatoes or broccoli rabe with garlic and oil.

4 (1-inch-thick) bone-in veal chops

2 teaspoons salt

6 tablespoons olive oil, divided

6 cloves garlic, smashed

Pepper, to taste

4 red bliss potatoes, cut into ½-inch-thick rounds

1 pound mushrooms, sliced

½ cup beef stock

6 hot cherry peppers in vinegar, cleaned, stemmed, and quartered

3 chives, each cut into 4 pieces

Season the veal chops generously with salt and let sit for 15 to 20 minutes. Rub chops with 3 tablespoons olive oil. Heat remaining 3 tablespoons oil in a frying pan set over medium-high heat, and sauté garlic for 2 to 3 minutes. Add pepper to taste. Add the veal chops to the pan and sear, about 4 minutes per side. Remove the chops and place them on a plate; set aside.

Reduce heat to medium and add the potatoes, browning them on each side for about 5 minutes. Add mushrooms and beef stock and sauté for another 5 minutes. Add cherry peppers and 2 tablespoons vinegar and toss in the chives. Increase heat to medium-high, add the chops back to the pan and cook for 3 or 4 minutes, turning the chops over once halfway through.

SERVES 4

ITALIAN VEAL CHOPS

What's better than veal chops, we ask? Italian veal chops, of course. Veal is a staple in an Italian family, but you have to be sure to make it just right so the meat is nice and tender. And trust me . . . we do. Cooking time and tenderness of the veal is most important, so stay as true to the recipe as possible and enjoy!

8 veal chops

Salt and pepper, to taste

2 tablespoons olive oil

4 cloves garlic, minced

1 (28-ounce) can plum San Marzano tomatoes

2 tablespoons fresh parsley

2 sprigs fresh oregano

Season the veal chops with salt and pepper. Heat olive oil in a sauté pan over medium heat, and brown the chops for 2 to 3 minutes per side. Transfer to a plate and set aside. In the same sauté pan, add garlic and cook until golden brown. Add tomatoes, parsley, and oregano. Increase heat to high and bring mixture to a boil, then reduce heat and simmer for 30 minutes. Add the veal back into the pan and simmer for 1½ hours more.

SERVES 6 TO 8

VEAL ROAST WITH POTATOES AND CARROTS

Pot roast, pork roast, veal roast . . . Mom made a lot of roasts growing up, but this is one of the favorites. Dad particularly likes veal, and when he returned home from his first "vacation," the whole family spent the day together making this for him. A nice, hearty meal is always important after time "away" from your family.

2 tablespoons olive oil

3 cloves garlic, chopped

2 tablespoons finely chopped fresh parsley

Salt and pepper, to taste

1 (2–3-pound) veal rump

3–4 potatoes, each cut into 8 pieces

5–6 carrots, peeled and left whole

½ cup dry white wine

Preheat oven to 350F.

In a bowl, mix together olive oil, garlic, parsley, salt, and pepper. Rub mixture on top of roast. Place the veal roast in a 9 × 13-inch baking dish, and surround with potatoes and carrots. Cook, covered with aluminum foil, for 40 minutes. Uncover, add the wine, and cook uncovered for another 20 minutes. Then uncover and cook for 20 minutes more.

SERVES 4

Lana's engagement party—
Veronica, Renee, Lana, and Jenn

Lana in her first home's kitchen

Renee and Lana at a family restaurant

PORK

REAL MEN EAT PORK

Mobsters hate pigs (otherwise known as cops)! It goes without saying that the men in our lives eat pork, but they won't talk to it. Real pork is a staple at most holidays, however, and we enjoy it so many different ways: Pork Chops with Sweet and Hot Cherry Peppers, Roast Pork with Potatoes and Fennel, Italian-Style Ribs and, most important, Sausage, Peppers, and Onions—a dish that brings us back to the heart of our youth at the San Gennaro feast. Pork was also our grandma's favorite. With these recipes, soon it will be yours, too!

PORK CHOPS WITH PEARS

Pork and pears? Pears and chops? Admit it—it seems odd, but you are intrigued. We promise you, though, after one bite you will be hooked for life! We enjoy making this culinary delight when entertaining new guests at home. Their expressions alone when they sink their teeth into each chop is worth the Amarone we pair with it.

¼ cup flour

Salt and pepper, to taste

4–6 pork chops

3 tablespoons olive oil

4 tablespoons salted butter

½ cup chicken stock

½ cup shallots and scallions, mixed

¼ cup heavy cream

1½ pears, sliced fairly thick

Combine flour, salt, pepper in a shallow plate. Dredge each pork chop in flour mixture until well coated. In a sauté pan, heat olive oil and butter over medium-high heat. Brown the pork chops, cooking them for 5 to 7 minutes per side. Remove the pork chops to a plate and set aside.

Add the chicken stock and the scallion mixture to the sauté pan, and stir. Slowly add in the heavy cream and cook until the sauce thickens. Add the pears and continue to cook until pears soften, 6 to 8 minutes. Pour the pear mixture over the pork chops and serve.

SERVES 4 TO 6

PORK CHOPS WITH SWEET AND HOT CHERRY PEPPERS

This dish flew out the door at Mangiare Tu. There was never enough pork chops to supply all of the demanding customers. The perfect combination of sweet and hot cherry peppers was reminiscent of the way Renee and Lana got along in the restaurant: Renee was sweet and Lana was always hot! One thing we learned over the years is that although we all share a love of food, we all have different temperaments and attitudes in the kitchen and toward business.

2 tablespoons olive oil

15 to 18 cloves garlic

4–6 (½-inch-thick) pork chops

¼ cup chicken stock

⅓ cup hot cherry peppers

1 cup jarred sliced sweet cherry peppers, plus a little juice from the jar

Salt and pepper, to taste

1 (14-ounce) box white rice, cooked according to package instructions, for serving

Heat olive oil in a sauté pan over medium-high heat, and cook garlic until softened. Add pork chops and brown for 5 to 6 minutes per side. Slowly add in the chicken stock, bringing it to a boil. Reduce heat to medium and add the hot cherry peppers and sweet cherry peppers plus juice. Season with salt and pepper. Spread the cooked rice out on a platter. Collect the juice from the frying pan and pour it over the rice. Place the pork chops and peppers over the rice and serve hot.

SERVES 4 TO 6

PORK CHOPS
WITH BALSAMIC VINEGAR

Anything with balsamic vinegar is delicious. There's nothing like the sweet yet tart flavor poured over any meat, especially pork. This is one of Grandma's favorites; we always loved to hear her say "bee nee gar" in her broken English-Italian accent.

6 pork chops

2 eggs

1 tablespoon milk

1 cup seasoned bread crumbs

3 tablespoons salted butter

2 tablespoons olive oil

3 cloves garlic

½ cup dry white wine

½ cup chicken stock

4 tablespoons balsamic vinegar

1 tablespoon diced fresh basil

Cut away any extra fat from the pork chops, and set the chops aside. Mix together eggs and milk in one bowl, and place bread crumbs in another bowl. Dip each pork chop in the egg mixture and then the bread crumbs, making sure to coat thoroughly. Heat butter and olive oil in a frying pan over medium heat add garlic, and cook until slightly browned, then add the pork chops. Brown well on both sides, 5 to 6 minutes per side. Pour wine over the chops and add the chicken stock. Reduce heat to low and cook for another 10 to 12 minutes, until almost all of the liquid has been absorbed. Drizzle the vinegar and basil over the chops and cook for another 2 to 3 minutes.

SERVES 4 TO 6

ITALIAN-STYLE RIBS

We like ribs just as much as the next guy, but they seemed to have a new meaning to us after the Season 3 reunion show when Ramona told Carla she wanted to use her ribs as toothpicks after she was finished eating her skin! Well, cannibalism is not in our blood, but we do love a good rack of ribs. Italian-style ribs are the best. Wait . . . isn't Carla Italian? Just kidding!

2 slabs lean pork ribs

Salt and pepper, to taste

½ cup finely chopped mushrooms

½ cup finely chopped artichokes preserved in oil

½ cup finely chopped mixed hot vegetable antipasto (jarred is fine)

1 (28-ounce) can whole San Marzano tomatoes

3 tablespoons finely chopped fresh basil

Preheat oven to 300F.

Season the ribs on both sides with salt and pepper. Place the ribs in a 9 × 13-inch baking pan and bake for 40 to 50 minutes, until rich brown in color. Combine the chopped vegetables with the tomatoes and basil and pour sauce over top of the ribs. Cover and bake for 1 hour. Uncover, reduce heat to 250F, and cook for 1 hour more, turning the ribs halfway through and basting them with the sauce. If the sauce gets too thick while cooking, add ½ cup water and stir into the sauce. Serve the ribs in pieces, with the sauce spooned on top.

SERVES 6

PORK TENDERLOIN WITH PRUNES AND PORT WINE

Prunes, prunes, prunes. All Grandma used to talk about was prunes . . . and now we know why! Prunes added to pork tenderloin with just the right amount of port wine makes the meat come alive with flavor. Mom would make this for us from time to time and we were never disappointed. Something about this home cooked meal brings back warm memories of Grandma. Serve this with Lana's Famous Salad (page 119) and you are sure to be a hit.

2½ pounds pork tenderloin

Salt and pepper, to taste

1½ tablespoons vegetable oil

½ cup port wine

½ cup chicken broth

15 pitted prunes

2 tablespoons salted butter

Preheat oven to 400F.

Season the tenderloin with salt and pepper. In a large frying pan, heat the oil over high heat. Add tenderloins and brown on all sides, about 3 minutes per side. Set the frying pan aside. Place pork tenderloin into a 9 × 13-inch baking pan and roast for 20 to 25 minutes, until the pork is done to medium. Place tenderloin on a cutting board, and let rest for 5 to 6 minutes.

Remove pan from oven. Separate the fat from the meat juices, being sure to get all the browned bits from the bottom of the pan. Add the juice and scrapings to the frying pan. Add the port wine and chicken broth, increase heat to medium-high, and bring mixture to a boil for 1 to 2 minutes, then reduce heat to medium. Once that comes to a boil, add the prunes. Reduce mixture to ½ cup, about 3 minutes. Turn off heat, add butter, and whisk until butter is thoroughly incorporated. Slice the meat and pour the prunes and sauce over the meat.

SERVES 4

SAUSAGE, PEPPERS, AND ONIONS

This dish is quick, beautiful, and healthy. It's an easy dish to make for a backyard party, and it's perfect eaten on a fresh piece of Italian bread. When we were young, Dad would take us to the San Gennaro feast in Little Italy every single year. We walked that feast like we owned it, often "winning" larger-than-life stuffed animals when we actually didn't win the game. The guy manning the stands would say, "Don't you worry, you take a prize anyway for trying so hard." We had so many prizes that we couldn't even carry them. But the best part of the day was when we stopped at Dad's friend's food stand and got a hero full of sausage, peppers, and onions before heading home. Dad used to always joke and say, "You don't like onions—pick 'em out. You don't like peppers—pick 'em out. You don't like sausage—get out. There are plenty of kids on the street I can replace you with."

3 tablespoons olive oil

1 head fresh garlic, peeled, each clove cut in half lengthwise

2 large sweet onions, sliced

3 pounds sausage (half hot and half sweet)

2 red peppers, cleaned and sliced

1 green pepper, cleaned and sliced

1 yellow pepper, cleaned and sliced

4 red potatoes, each cut into 8 pieces (optional)

Preheat oven to 375F.

Heat olive oil in a sauté pan over medium heat, and sauté garlic and onion until browned. Add sausages and brown, about 2 minutes per side, then remove from heat and let cool. Place the sausage mixture in a 9 × 13-inch baking pan. Add the peppers and potatoes, if using, and cover with aluminum foil. Bake for 30 to 40 minutes, stirring halfway through. Uncover and bake for an additional 30 minutes, until golden brown.

SERVES 6

ROAST PORK WITH POTATOES AND FENNEL

Another way to enjoy a pork roast is with the delicious flavors of fennel. The flavors complement each other so perfectly, you won't be disappointed. Plus, a little Italian liqueur never hurt anybody. In fact, Dad always had an extra shot on the side when making this dish!

½ cup olive oil, divided

2 tablespoons Sambuca

4 large cloves garlic, minced

2 tablespoons finely chopped fresh rosemary

Salt and pepper, to taste

1 (3-pound) boneless pork loin (ask the butcher to leave ¼-inch fat on the top)

1½ pounds small yellow potatoes (about 10), halved

2 medium sweet onions, halved and cut into ¼-inch slices

1 large fennel bulb, stalks cut off and bulb quartered and cut lengthwise into ¼-inch slices

1½ cups chicken stock

¾ cup dry white wine

In a small bowl, mix ¼ cup olive oil and Sambuca with the garlic, rosemary, salt, and pepper until a paste forms; set aside. Pat the pork loin dry with paper towels. Rub the paste over the entire roast. Cover and refrigerate overnight.

Preheat oven to 400F.

Arrange the potatoes, onions, and fennel in a roasting pan, add salt, pepper, and remaining ¼ cup olive oil. Cook, turning occasionally, until vegetables are almost tender (test with a fork), about 35 minutes.

Reduce oven temperature to 300F. Put the pork loin into the pan, fat side up, and pour the juice from the meat on top of the vegetables. Add chicken stock and the wine, and roast, basting the meat and vegetables occasionally, about 2 hours.

Separate the fat from the juices and, in a frying pan, simmer the juice until it reduces, 3 to 5 minutes. Slice the pork loin and pour the juice over the pork. Arrange the sliced pork on a platter with the vegetables.

SERVES 4

7

SIDES

WE GOT A SIDE JOB FOR YA

Where we grew up, everyone always had a side job, like being a bookie or something. And a side piece—we'll leave that one alone; however, we have plenty of side jobs to offer here! There are so many delicious side dishes you can make to accompany your meals and we wanted to share some of our favorites with you—Zucchini with Garlic and Oil, Ricotta Cheese Mashed Potatoes, String Beans Oreganata, Roasted Potatoes, Sicilian Rice Balls, and so much more. Just mix and match these with your favorite entrées from the book—only the best for you when you're with us!

STRING BEAN SALAD WITH RED POTATOES AND RED ONIONS

Renee was skinny as a string bean growing up, and that became her nickname. We called her that so often that she refused to eat them at all. But Jennifer and Lana love to make this quick dish as a delicious side to steaks and meats.

1 pound red potatoes, halved

1 pound green beans, trimmed

1 small red onion, thinly sliced

2 cloves garlic, minced

Salt and pepper, to taste

3 tablespoons balsamic vinegar

2 tablespoons fresh parsley, chopped

5 tablespoons olive oil

In a large pot filled with cold water, add the potatoes, bring to a boil, and cook for 20 to 30 minutes until the potatoes are fork-tender. Drain and set aside in a bowl. In the same pot, boil more water and add the green beans. Cook them for 10 to 12 minutes, drain, and add them to the bowl with the potatoes. Add the red onion and season with garlic, salt, pepper, and vinegar. Toss to combine. Add the fresh parsley and olive oil, and stir again. Serve at room temperature.

SERVES 4 TO 6

LANA'S FAMOUS SALAD

For the salad course, forget your mundane iceberg lettuce. Lana's idea of a salad has an array of herbs and spices that will wake up your salivary glands! This salad is colorful, with lots of ingredients—the more the merrier, says Lana. She adds everything from chunks of blue cheese to chickpeas to chow mein noodles, which add a nice bit of crunch to the salad. Lana's Famous Salad is a family favorite. Jennifer serves it at all of her events, and it always receives rave reviews. To make this into a heartier main dish, add some sliced beef, chicken, or shrimp.

⅓ cup olive oil

½ cup balsamic vinegar

2–3 squeezes balsamic glaze

1½ teaspoons onion powder

¾ teaspoon garlic powder

Salt and pepper, to taste

1 head romaine lettuce, washed and cut into bite-size pieces

2 cups arugula

1 cup iceberg lettuce

1 cup baby spinach

¼ cup red onion, thinly sliced

¼ cup crumbled blue cheese

¼ cup chickpeas

½ cup canned, sliced beets

¼ cup roasted red peppers

¼ cup shredded mozzarella cheese

¼ cup crunchy chow mein noodles (optional)

To make the dressing, whisk together in a bowl the olive oil, balsamic vinegar, and balsamic glaze. Whisk in the onion powder, garlic powder, and salt and pepper. Toss the rest of the ingredients together with the dressing, and serve.

SERVES 4 TO 6

STRING BEANS OREGANATA

"Crumbs! Crumbs! I hate crumbs! All they do is leave crumbs!" In Season 2, there's an episode where Renee goes off the deep end about crumbs being left in her kitchen by AJ. This scene made national headlines. Renee became the subject of many spoofs, and the episode will live on in the minds of Mob Wives fans forever. What they don't know is that some of the crumbs that were left on the floor and counter that night came from the bread crumbs on the String Beans Oreganata! Each and every time we make this dish, we all run around the house screaming, "Crumbs, crumbs, we hate crumbs!"

1½ pounds string beans

¼ cup olive oil

8–10 cloves garlic

Salt and pepper, to taste

⅓ cup seasoned bread crumbs

¼ cup grated Pecorino-Romano cheese

Fill a 2-quart saucepan three-quarters full with water and bring to a boil. Add string beans and cook them until tender but not mushy, 5 to 6 minutes. Drain and set aside. In a sauté pan, heat the olive oil over medium heat. Add garlic, salt, and pepper, to taste, and then add the string beans. Add the bread crumbs and grated cheese, and toss to coat the string beans. Keep cooking over medium heat, tossing until bread crumbs are golden brown. Remove and serve hot.

SERVES 4

ESCAROLE AND BEANS

For this delicious dish, you have to make sure to thoroughly clean the escarole because it gets "sandy" and can mess up the whole recipe if not cleaned properly. It's a traditional dish served at lots of restaurants, even those that are not Italian. Who doesn't love this? To make this a main dish (and to add some extra spice), grill some sausages and serve the escarole and beans over them. Or, if you'd like to make it soupier, add more chicken stock and some pasta. The possibilities with this dish are endless!

2 large bunches escarole

½ cup olive oil

5–6 cloves garlic, cut into large pieces

1 cup chicken stock

Salt and pepper, to taste

½ teaspoon crushed red pepper (optional)

2 (15-ounce) cans cannellini beans, divided

½ cup grated Pecorino-Romano cheese

Cut the tough root off the escarole and remove any damaged outside layers. Peel back the leaves and wash the escarole well under cold water. Drain well in a strainer, then cut escarole into 2-inch pieces. Heat the oil in a 2-quart saucepan over medium-high heat and sauté garlic until light brown. Add the chicken stock, escarole, salt, pepper, and red pepper, if using, and bring to a boil for 2 to 3 minutes. Reduce heat to medium-low and add 1 can of beans. Place remaining beans into a blender and blend on medium speed for 2 minutes. Scoop the mixture out with a spatula and add the beans to pot. Add the grated cheese, stir to combine, and simmer for 10 to 12 minutes.

SERVES 4

ROASTED BEETS WITH APPLES AND GOAT CHEESE

Beets are by far our prized vegetable, and Granny Smith apples have a sweetness like no other. When both are combined with goat cheese, it brings out a party of flavors that's an absolute explosion in your mouth. This is best served with a great rib-eye steak.

10–12 medium-sized red beets

⅓ cup extra virgin olive oil

⅓ cup good balsamic vinegar

½ teaspoon salt

Black pepper, to taste

1 medium-sized tart, crisp apple, such as Granny Smith

½ cup slightly aged goat cheese

Preheat oven to 400F.

Scrub the beets and prick each several times with a fork. Put them all in a shallow baking dish, uncovered, and add ⅛-inch water to bottom of pan. Roast the beets—the water will actually steam them a bit first—until they are shriveled, dark, and caramelized outside, and tender all the way through (when poked with a knife), 1 to 1½ hours, depending on size. Remove from oven and let cool completely.

Wearing gloves so as not to stain your hands, peel the cooled beets, removing all the skin, the stem base, and the root tip. Cut into wedges, and place in a large mixing bowl. In a separate bowl, mix together the oil, vinegar, salt, and pepper to taste. Drizzle dressing over the beets, and toss to combine. Core and slice the apple into thin matchsticks. Fold apple pieces into beets. Arrange on a serving platter or portion mixture onto salad plates, and crumble goat cheese on top just before serving.

SERVES 4

ZUCCHINI WITH GARLIC AND OIL

As you can see, everything tastes better with garlic and oil. If you don't believe us, then ask our grandma Nora. She'd tell you if it didn't have garlic and oil then you don't put it on the table. This dish consists of beautiful yellow or green zucchini sautéed just right . . . your kids will forget they are eating a vegetable.

4 tablespoons olive oil

6–8 cloves garlic

½ cup chicken stock

4 zucchini, peeled and sliced lengthwise, then cut into ½-inch-thick slices

Salt and pepper, to taste

In a sauté pan, heat olive oil over medium heat and sauté garlic until slightly brown. Add chicken stock and cook for 5 minutes more. Add the zucchini, salt, and pepper, tossing occasionally. Cover the pan for 10 minutes, checking often, until the zucchini gets tender. If it gets too dry, add a little water.

SERVES 4

ASPARAGUS RISOTTO

Some think that risotto is just a fancy way to say rice in Italian. Well, it basically is! Risotto is a creamier version than your traditional American dry rice; we like to add just about any vegetable to it, especially asparagus. The best part about this dish is that it can paired with fish, meat, or even eaten alone as the main course. Either way, you will always be satisfied.

4 cups vegetable or chicken broth

2 tablespoons olive oil

2 onions, chopped

1 cup white rice

2 pounds asparagus, cut into 2-inch pieces

2 tablespoons salted or unsalted butter

½ cup grated Parmigiano-Reggiano cheese

Salt and pepper, to taste

In a small saucepan, bring the broth to a simmer. Heat the olive oil in a large pot over medium heat. Add onions and rice and cook, stirring, until rice is browned, about 5 minutes. Stir in broth, ½ cup at a time, and cook, stirring constantly, until almost all the broth is absorbed before adding more, until rice is al dente, about 20 minutes; add hot water if you need more liquid. About 5 minutes before rice is done, add asparagus, butter, cheese, salt, and pepper, and cook until asparagus is crisp-tender.

SERVES 4

RICOTTA CHEESE MASHED POTATOES

Like we said before, anything with cheese is the best. What better way, however, to "Italianize" an American staple like mashed potatoes than to add some creamy ricotta cheese? This is wonderful served with Chicken Marsala (page 68).

2 pounds Yukon gold potatoes

Salt and pepper, to taste

1½ cups fresh ricotta cheese

½ cup milk

½ stick butter

2 cups mozzarella cheese, shredded

1 cup grated Parmigiano-Reggiano cheese

Place potatoes in a large pot with enough water to cover, bring to a boil, and cook until soft, 20 to 30 minutes, until a fork easily pierces the potato skin.

Preheat oven to 350F.

Drain potatoes, place into a large bowl, and mash using a hand-held mixer. Add salt, pepper, ricotta cheese, milk, and butter and mash again. Place potatoes into a 9 × 13-inch baking dish. Sprinkle the shredded mozzarella cheese and grated cheese on top, and bake for 15 to 20 minutes.

SERVES 6 TO 8

BROCCOLI RABE WITH GARLIC AND OIL

If this side dish had a soundtrack, it would be The Omen. *This amazing vegetable is the kryptonite of every Goodfella and Godfather out there. No Italian can resist when it hits the table, and you should be prepared to succumb to its greatness. Our family eats this by the plateful— and so will yours tonight, so make sure you made enough for the whole neighborhood! The best thing is that it can be served as a side to meats or chicken, or even better, any leftovers can be made into a frittata. To make this more of a meal, you can grill up some sausage and serve it alongside the broccoli rabe.*

2 bunches broccoli rabe, ends cut

4 tablespoons olive oil

8–10 cloves garlic, cut into chunks

Salt and pepper, to taste

½ tablespoon crushed red pepper flakes

½ cup chicken stock, divided

Fill a 3-quart saucepan with water, bring to a boil, and cook broccoli rabe for 3 minutes. Drain and set aside. Heat olive oil in a large pan over medium heat, and sauté garlic until softened. Add salt, pepper, and red pepper flakes. Add ¼ cup chicken stock and bring to a boil; add broccoli rabe. Reduce heat to medium and add remaining ¼ cup chicken stock. Cook until tender, 6 to 8 minutes.

SERVES 4

SWEET PEAS WITH PROSCIUTTO

This is quick and easy, with the perfect juxtaposition of sweet and salty flavors. It's a fast Italian side that Dad whipped up when he was in the kitchen, to accompany a great meal. It can be served alone as a side or mixed together with small or medium pasta shells for an amazing pasta dish.

¼ cup olive oil

2 ounces prosciutto, chopped into bite-size pieces

1 large sweet onion, minced

¼ cup chicken stock, plus more for serving

1 (12-ounce) package sweet peas (or 1 can sweet peas)

Salt and pepper, to taste

1 pound small shell pasta, cooked according to package instructions, for serving (optional)

1 cup grated Parmigiano-Reggiano cheese (optional)

In a large frying pan over medium heat, heat the olive oil for 1 to 2 minutes, and then add the prosciutto and onion. Cook until the onion is soft and the prosciutto begins to crisp, 6 to 8 minutes. Add the chicken stock, increase heat, and bring to a boil. Cook for 2 to 3 minutes more. Add the peas and cook, tossing, until hot, about 3 minutes. Season with salt and pepper.

If desired, add a little more chicken stock; serve with small shell pasta and top with grated cheese.

SERVES 4

CARAMELIZED FENNEL AND ONIONS

What's better than caramelized onions? The answer: caramelized onions with fennel! We throw this on any plain meat and call it a meal. You can also add this on top of a white pizza for a twist, or just enjoy plain as a side dish.

¼ cup olive oil

1 tablespoon butter

2 large fennel bulbs, cut into ¼-inch-thick slices

3 large onions, halved then sliced

Salt and pepper, to taste

½ cup grated Parmigiano-Reggiano cheese

2 tablespoons chopped fresh parsley

1 teaspoon lemon zest

2 teaspoons lemon juice

Heat the olive oil and butter in a large pan on medium-high heat. Add the sliced fennel and onions and stir to coat. Heat while stirring occasionally. Cook for 15 minutes, stirring occasionally. Sprinkle fennel with salt and pepper. Lower the temperature to medium. You want to strike a balance between allowing the pan to get hot enough so that the onions and fennel will caramelize (you will see them start to brown) and burning them. If it looks like they are starting to burn, add a couple tablespoons of water to the pan to keep the onions and fennel from drying out. Continue to stir occasionally, scraping up any browned bits from the bottom of the pan. Cook for another 30 minutes to 1 hour, depending on how caramelized you want your mixture to be. The longer you cook, the more caramelized and browned they will become. When ready to serve, remove from heat and toss in cheese, chopped parsley, lemon zest, and lemon juice.

SERVES 4

ROASTED POTATOES

Roasted potatoes go with everything. Making Chicken Parmesan? Pair it with these. Veal Piccata? Meat loaf? You name it—it all goes perfectly with potatoes roasted to perfection.

2 pounds red skinned potatoes,
cut in 1½- to 2-inch chunks

1 large sweet onion, sliced

4–5 cloves garlic, smashed

1 teaspoon salt

¼ teaspoon black pepper

2 teaspoons parsley

¼ cup olive oil

2 tablespoons salted butter

Preheat oven to 400F.

Combine all of the ingredients in a large bowl or food storage bag; toss to coat thoroughly. Arrange in a 9 × 13-inch baking pan and bake for 30 to 40 minutes, turning once halfway through, until potatoes are tender and nicely browned.

SERVES 4 TO 6

LANA'S FAMOUS GRILLED CORN ON THE COB

One would never expect to eat corn on the cob with provolone and anchovies but this version of grilled corn is to die for. Lana's ex-husband, John, made this for us at every family barbecue and, since then, we've all learned how to make it to perfection.

6 ears corn, husks on

5 tablespoons olive oil

8–10 cloves garlic, chopped

2 anchovy fillets, packed in olive oil

4 long hot peppers, sliced into ½-inch slices

½ cup (1 stick) salted butter

Salt and pepper, to taste

¼ pound sharp provolone, cut into chunks

Wash the outside of the corn, remove silk, and peel back one layer on the outside. Soak the corn in warm water 15 to 20 minutes. Heat the olive oil in a large frying pan over medium heat, and sauté garlic and anchovies, 5 to 6 minutes. Add the hot peppers, turning and cooking on all sides until they change to a darker-color green, 4 to 5 minutes more. Transfer mixture to a large bowl, and add butter, and salt and pepper to taste.

Heat a grill to high. Grill corn, turning until each side is burned and the leaves become black, about 10 minutes per side. Spray the corncobs with some water while they're on the grill. Remove each cob when finished and leave in the husks to keep warm. After they are all grilled, pull back the husks and cut each cob into 1½-inch circles. Add them to the anchovy mixture of garlic, oil, and anchovies. Mix well, coating all of the corn. Cover the bowl and set aside for 10 minutes, then stir mixture again. Top with provolone and serve hot.

SERVES 6

LANA'S MEATBALLS

Of the three of us, Renee is perhaps the most experimental in the kitchen. One time she didn't have bread or bread crumbs to make her meatballs and, after thinking long and hard, she ended up using potato chips instead. We laughed and mocked her all day long but, honestly, we couldn't believe how delicious they turned out. That's high praise indeed: meatballs are a hot commodity in the Graziano family, considering someone once got stabbed with a fork for trying to steal the last one! This makes us wonder . . . is it the meatball or the Italian nature that brings out such aggression? During Season 1, Renee made an Italian meal for all the girls, including meatballs, and she and Carla ended up rolling around on the floor in a hair-pulling match! We bet you that Carla stole the last meatball.

1½ pounds ground lean beef

¾ pound ground veal

¾ pound ground pork

3 large eggs

2 cups grated Pecorino-Romano cheese

6–8 basil leaves, chopped up

4 cloves garlic, peeled and minced very fine

Salt and pepper, to taste

½–¾ 16-ounce loaf Italian bread

1 cup vegetable oil

Combine the beef, veal, and pork in a large bowl. Add eggs, grated cheese, basil, garlic, salt, and pepper. Run the Italian bread under warm water and squeeze out the excess water. Break the bread into small pieces and add it to the meat mixture. Combine ingredients using your hands, and shape mixture into 2-inch balls. Heat vegetable oil in a large frying pan set over medium-high heat. When the oil is very hot but not smoking, fry the meatballs in batches until the bottom half of each meatball is very brown and crispy, 4 to 5 minutes. Turn and cook the meatballs 4 to 5 minutes on each side. Remove from heat and drain on paper towels.

MAKES ABOUT 20 TO 25 MEATBALLS

A GUIDE TO SNEAKING BALLS INTO PRISON

It's an unfortunate truth of the lifestyle that the men mostly go to jail. But they still never want to miss Sunday dinner. So the women pack up the meatballs, the sauces, the sopressata, the mozzarella, and then they sneak it into prison.

The best method of sneaking meatballs into prison: Get a bag of potato chips from the prison vending machine, go outside the building, empty out the chips, and put the meatballs in the bag, and then go back in. This only works when sneaking balls into a federal camp. Otherwise, leave the goods on the side of the road and try to get a guard to bring it in. Offer him some meatballs for his effort.

—Renee Graziano

SICILIAN RICE BALLS

There's something about Sicilians and their balls! Sicilian men are tough guys who aren't afraid of anything. But give them one of these rice balls and they will weaken in their knees. Stuffed to perfection, these rice balls are always moist. We eat these cold for breakfast or piping-hot for lunch and dinner.

1 medium onion, finely chopped

2–3 cloves garlic, minced

1 pound lean ground beef

1 pound white rice

½ cup salted butter, softened

1 cup grated Pecorino-Romano cheese

2 eggs

1 tablespoon milk

2 cups seasoned bread crumbs

Salt and pepper, to taste

1 cup vegetable oil, for frying

Sauté onion, garlic, and ground beef over medium heat until brown, 6 to 8 minutes. After cooking, drain off excess juices. Set aside.

Cook rice according to package instructions. Stir in butter and grated cheese, and set aside to cool. To make the rice balls: put a heaping serving spoon of rice in the palm of your hand. Make a hole in the rice with your finger and fill it with some of the meat mixture, then top with another spoonful of rice. Form it into a ball with your hands. Mix the egg and milk in one bowl, and put the bread crumbs, salt, and pepper in another. Dip each ball in egg and then in the bread crumbs, coating each ball. Place the balls in the refrigerator for 30 minutes; this will help them keep their shape during frying. In a frying pan, heat the vegetable oil over medium-high heat until it starts to bubble, then start adding in the rice balls. Brown them on all sides, 4 to 5 minutes.

MAKES 5 OR 6 LARGE RICE BALLS

Happy 1st Anniversary!

Lana (center) and her son Anthony (right)
with the staff of Mangiare Tu

ITALIAN SPECIALTIES

ARE YOU A SPECIALIST?

Everyone has a specialty—and in the mob there are many—construction, sanitation, sports betting, you name it. Some families allegedly control concrete; it has also been said that some families control the fish market, who knows. But what we do know is that in our family, our specialty is food. This chapter includes dishes we consider unique in Italian cuisine that can be served as a side, an appetizer, or a whole meal. Some can be served for breakfast and some for dinner—some even both. The recipes in this section are common among most Italian families, restaurants, and cookbooks, so we wanted to be sure to include them. Ricotta and Eggs with Toasted Italian Bread, Zucchini Frittata, Italian Cheesy Garlic Bread, Stuffed Artichokes, Caesar Salad, and Italian Wedding Soup are just a few. *Mangia* and *Buon appetito!*

ITALIAN CHEESY GARLIC BREAD

Garlic, cheese, and bread all together in one: an Italian's dream. This can be a starter to any meal and we guarantee there won't be a piece left over. Kick it up a notch and throw on some fresh anchovies before baking to give it an authentic Sicilian flavor. Anthony, Lana's son, is notorious for making this version!

1 loaf Italian bread

1 cup grated Pecorino-Romano cheese

½ cup grated Fontina cheese

5–6 cloves garlic, finely minced

6–8 fresh basil leaves, chopped

½ teaspoon fresh parsley, chopped

Salt and pepper, to taste

2 tablespoons salted butter, softened

2–3 tablespoons olive oil

Preheat oven to 350F. Line a baking sheet with tin foil and set aside.

Cut the Italian bread down the middle, and set aside. In a medium-sized bowl, combine remaining ingredients except olive oil. Drizzle olive oil down both sides of the Italian bread. Spread cheese mixture evenly onto bread, and place bread on prepared baking sheet. Bake for 8 to 10 minutes, and then place under the broiler for 2 minutes, until very crispy.

SERVES 6

RICOTTA AND EGGS WITH TOASTED ITALIAN BREAD

When Lana owned Mangiare Tu and lived in "the big house," as we liked to call it (and we don't mean "the slammer"), the entire family used to sleep over on weekends and spend time together. Mom, Dad, Renee, AJ, Jennifer, Justin, Anthony, John, Sonni, Michelle, Gabrielle, Alexis, Li'l John, Marilyn, and Jamie . . . we were all there. Lana's ex-husband, John, and her kids would wake up extra early and start breakfast for everyone. Sonni and Gab would cut up the fruit and John would butter the bread, while Anthony helped their father with the Ricotta and Eggs. John made it the best and, although they are no longer together, he's still part of the family and so is the tradition. The kids still go over to his house every now and again for this specialty, which was passed down to him from his mother, Rosie, while the rest of the family enjoys it with Lana, who has mastered the dish.

1 loaf crusty Italian bread, sliced into 6 pieces

2–3 tablespoons salted butter, plus additional for buttering bread

1 pint whole-milk ricotta

4 eggs

Toast the Italian bread, butter it, and set aside. In an oven-safe frying pan, melt butter over medium heat, then add the ricotta. Cook the ricotta until all the water has been released, 35 to 45 minutes, turning cheese frequently with a spatula to keep it from burning. During the last 8 to 10 minutes, the bottom of the ricotta will begin to brown. Once you see that it's browning, crack the eggs on top. Cook the eggs, sunny side up, for 5 minutes. Turn the oven to the broil setting, place the frying pan on the top shelf of the oven and broil the tops of the eggs. Take care not to burn them—you want to see the eggs get slightly brown in color. After the pan has cooled down, invert the frying pan onto a plate and cut into pie slices. Toast the bread and serve.

SERVES 4

ZUCCHINI FRITTATA

What happens when you made too much Zucchini with Garlic and Oil and have some left over from dinner? You combine it with eggs and you've got breakfast. The good thing is that you can make a frittata with just about any vegetable—spinach, broccoli, asparagus—and you can add in meats and mozzarella cheese. But, as always, zucchini is one of our favorites. Jennifer's son went to school around the block from Mom's house, and every morning after Jennifer dropped him off, she would call Mom to ask her what vegetables were left over for Mom to make a frittata with. Soon we were all headed to Mom's house for breakfast! This is also great as a side dish, and it also stands alone as a quick and healthy snack.

4 small zucchini

4 tablespoons olive oil, divided

6 cloves garlic, minced

½ sweet onion, diced

8 large eggs, plus 2 egg whites

1 cup grated Parmigiano-Reggiano cheese

1 cup shredded mozzarella cheese

Salt and pepper, to taste

Preheat oven to 375F.

Peel zucchini and slice lengthwise down the middle, and then cut each one into ½-inch slices. Heat 2 tablespoons olive oil in a nonstick pan set over medium heat. Cook the garlic and onion until light brown, and then add the zucchini and cook for 6 to 8 minutes. The zucchini should be soft and slightly brown. Set aside.

Crack the eggs into a medium-sized bowl and whisk until the yolks and whites are combined. Add half the grated cheese and the salt and pepper. Heat remaining 2 tablespoons olive oil in a nonstick, oven-safe frying pan. Add the egg mixture and the zucchini. Cook on medium heat until the egg mixture is golden on the top, 5 to 10 minutes. Sprinkle the rest of the grated cheese and mozzarella on top and put the pan in the oven. Bake for 5 to 7 minutes, until the frittata is cooked through. You can check for doneness by sticking a knife into the frittata. If the knife comes out wet, cook the frittata for 2 to 3 minutes more. Cut the frittata into wedges and serve.

SERVES 6

EGGPLANT ROLLATINI

Eggplant rollatini is another staple in most Italian restaurants and households, and something that Jennifer orders each time we go out to eat. Of course she likes it piping-hot with extra cheese. Lana likes it cold on Italian bread. Whatever your preference, you're gonna love this recipe.

2 tablespoons olive oil

1 small onion, diced

2 cloves garlic, diced

Salt and pepper, to taste

1 (28-ounce) can crushed San Marzano tomatoes

2 cups seasoned bread crumbs

1 cup grated Pecorino-Romano cheese

3 large eggs, plus 2 egg yolks, divided

1 tablespoon milk

2 large eggplants, sliced lengthwise (14–16 slices)

1 cup vegetable oil

1 (15-ounce) container whole-milk ricotta

2 cups grated mozzarella

3 tablespoons fresh basil, minced

Preheat oven to 450F.

Heat olive oil in a sauté pan over medium heat, and add the onion, garlic, salt, and pepper, and cook until the garlic is slightly brown. Add tomatoes and sauté over low to medium heat for 30 to 40 minutes. Turn off the heat and allow sauce to cool. In a bowl, combine bread crumbs and grated cheese. In another bowl beat together eggs and milk.

Dip each piece of eggplant into egg mixture and then in the bread crumbs. Make sure each piece is thoroughly coated. In a frying pan over medium heat, heat vegetable oil and fry each piece, cooking until golden brown, 3 to 4 minutes per side. Remove and set on paper towels to absorb the excess oil.

In a bowl combine ricotta, mozzarella, basil, and two egg yolks, and mix well. Take each piece of eggplant, place 1½ to 2 tablespoons ricotta mixture on each, and roll each one up. Spread 1 cup sauce in a baking dish large enough to hold rollatini in a single layer. Place rollatini on top of sauce, about ½ inch apart. Top each off with 1 tablespoon sauce. Bake for 20 to 25 minutes.

SERVES 6 TO 8

STUFFED ZUCCHINI

Zucchini in garlic and oil. Zucchini with pasta. Zucchini, zucchini, zucchini! We can't get enough of zucchini. But what we haven't told you about yet is our delicious stuffed zucchini. We take a whole zucchini and cut it in half, stuff it, and bake it. It's a new way to enjoy this delicious and nutritious vegetable.

5–6 zucchini, peeled and sliced lengthwise

½ cup olive oil, divided

2 cloves garlic, minced

1 small onion, diced

½ pound ground beef

½ cup grated Pecorino-Romano cheese

¼ cup fresh parsley, minced

½ cup seasoned bread crumbs

Salt and pepper, to taste

2 egg yolks

5–6 slices mozzarella, cut in half

Preheat oven to 350F. Oil a baking sheet with ¼ cup olive oil, and set aside.

Scoop out insides of zucchini, place in a bowl, and set aside. In a frying pan set over medium heat, heat remaining ¼ cup olive oil. Sauté garlic and onion for 3 to 4 minutes, until onions are translucent, then add ground beef. Cook until browned, 5 to 6 minutes, and then drain off all the liquid. Let cool and add that to the bowl with zucchini pulp. Add grated cheese, parsley, salt, and pepper. Mix well and add the egg yolks; mix again.

Fill each zucchini half with meat mixture and top with mozzarella. Place the zucchini on prepared baking sheet. Bake for 20 minutes, until the mozzarella starts to bubble. If it's not bubbling, bake for another 5 or 10 minutes.

SERVES 6 TO 8

CHOP MEAT-STUFFED RED PEPPERS

We have peppers and we're stuffing them with meat! This is a delicious combination of flavors for a perfect Italian starter or side dish. The colorful red pepper and the hearty meat make for a delicious treat.

1 pound ground beef

4 tablespoons olive oil

1 large sweet onion

3 cloves garlic, chopped

4–5 fresh plum tomatoes, diced

Salt and pepper, to taste

2 tablespoons finely chopped fresh basil

1 cup cooked instant rice

½ cup grated Pecorino-Romano cheese

1 (7-ounce) package shredded whole-milk mozzarella cheese, divided

4 large red or yellow bell peppers, tops removed and insides scooped out

4 tablespoons water, divided

Preheat oven to 350F.

Cook the rice according to package instructions and set aside. In a large frying pan over medium-high heat, sauté the ground beef and cook for 5 to 6 minutes; using a wooden fork break up the meat. Drain all the oil from the pan and place the meat into a bowl. Don't worry if the meat isn't cooked all the way. Set aside.

Wash the frying pan; heat olive oil over medium heat and sauté onions and garlic until onion is translucent, 4 to 5 minutes. Add tomatoes, salt, pepper, and basil, and continue to cook for 7 to 8 minutes. Remove from heat and add to meat. Stir in the rice and grated cheese and half of the cheese and mix well. Stuff the peppers with the meat mixture, and add 1 tablespoon water to each pepper on top of the meat, then top with remaining mozzarella. Place the peppers in a 9 × 13-inch baking pan, and pour ¼ cup water into bottom of pan. Bake for 20 minutes, then turn oven to broil and broil for 3 minutes, until cheese is browned and melted.

SERVES 4

STUFFED ZUCCHINI FLOWERS

We loved zucchini flowers as children, and we would walk to the fruit stand with Dad to pick some up in Heartland Village, where we lived. But we truly started to love them when another one of our favorite Brooklyn restaurants, Areos, added them to their menu. This place was a trendy Brooklyn delight where anyone who was anyone went to eat on a Thursday night. You bet we were there ordering the stuffed zucchini flowers special every week.

10–12 zucchini flowers (no stems)

1 cup flour

¼ teaspoon baking soda

Salt and pepper, to taste

¾ cup club soda

1 cup whole-milk ricotta

1 egg yolk

⅓ cup grated Pecorino-Romano cheese

8 fresh basil leaves, minced, divided

½ cup vegetable oil

6 fresh plum tomatoes, diced

2 cloves garlic, minced fine

3 tablespoons olive oil

Wash the flowers thoroughly with cold water, and set on a paper towel to air-dry. In another bowl, whisk together flour, baking soda, salt, and pepper. Slowly whisk in club soda. The mixture should be like a crêpe batter; set aside. In another bowl, mix together ricotta, egg yolk, grated cheese, and half of the basil. Mix well. In another bowl, combine tomatoes, garlic, and olive oil, and set aside.

Open the zucchini flowers by gently pulling down some of the petals. Add the ricotta filling into the middle, and pull the petals back in place. Twist the top of the petals together with your fingers to close them up. Dip each flower into the batter, coating thoroughly. In a frying pan, heat vegetable oil over medium-high heat. Once heated, add each flower and slightly brown on each side. Evenly divide tomato mixture on top of flowers.

If you're not crazy about cold tomato salad, you can sauté the tomatoes in garlic and olive oil for 4 to 6 minutes over medium heat and serve those on top of the stuffed flowers.

SERVES 6

STUFFED ARTICHOKES

This recipe has caused more death threats and injuries than all the victims in mob movies combined. For argument's sake, only one artichoke is made per family member but there never seems to be enough. Jennifer is notorious for hiding and bringing home at least one extra for herself. Arti-"choke"—more like "I'll choke you out if you have more than one" is our family motto. Make sure you sit next to someone who only eats a few leaves and is done.

4 large artichokes

½ cup olive oil, divided

8 cloves garlic, finely diced

1 large sweet onion, chopped

Salt and pepper to taste

1¾ cups seasoned bread crumbs

Juice of 1 lemon

½ cup fresh parsley, finely chopped

½ stick butter

½ cup chicken stock

1 cup grated cheese

4 tablespoons salted butter

2 cups water

Preheat oven to 425F.

Using a serrated knife, cut off artichoke stems so that the artichokes are flat on the bottom. Cut the tips off of the leaves and pull off tough outermost leaves. Open the artichoke leaves with your thumbs to make room for stuffing, then set aside.

In a small pot, heat ¼ cup olive oil over medium heat and add the garlic, onions, salt, and pepper. Sauté until garlic is slightly brown and onions are translucent. Add the bread crumbs, lemon juice, parsley, ½ stick of butter, chicken stock, and grated cheese. Stir so that the bread crumbs don't stick or burn, 3 to 4 minutes, until bread crumbs are slightly browned.

Make sure the mixture is a little wet and pasty. Transfer to a bowl to cool and set aside.

Stuff one artichoke at a time with the bread crumb mixture, working it in between leaves.

Put the stuffed artichokes into a baking dish. Drizzle the remaining ¼ cup olive oil over the artichokes, and top each one with 1 tablespoon butter.

Boil water, then pour into a baking pan to reach 2 to 3 inches. Place artichokes in the pan, cover with foil, and bake for 30 minutes. Remove the foil, and with a large spoon, scoop up the juice and pour it over each artichoke, then continue to bake without foil for another 40 to 45 minutes, until a knife easily slides into the base of an artichoke. Turn oven to broil. Place artichokes under the broiler for 2 to 3 minutes, until tops are crispy and brown.

SERVES 4

STUFFED SPINACH BREAD

Nobody loves her bread more than Mom; we always found her sneaking a piece in the corner of the kitchen in between meals. But what she loves more than anything is our Stuffed Spinach Bread. This is an old Italian recipe, learned and perfected by all of us. The smell of bread baking in the oven is enough to excite you, but when you cut it up and the mozzarella is dripping out, you can't help but eat it piping hot. The good news is you can stuff bread with just about anything. Substitute in broccoli rabe, prosciutto, you name it. It's always a great way to start or end a meal.

3–4 tablespoons olive oil

1 sweet onion, diced

1 (10-ounce) package frozen chopped spinach, thawed

Salt and pepper, to taste

¼ teaspoon crushed red pepper flakes

1½ cups whole-milk shredded mozzarella

⅓ cup grated Parmigiano-Reggiano cheese

¼ cup flour

1 pound ball pizza dough

1 egg white

Preheat oven to 350F. Spray a cookie sheet with nonstick cooking spray, and set aside.

In a sauté pan, heat the olive oil over medium heat and cook onion until translucent. Add the spinach to the pan and stir, then add the salt, pepper, and crushed red pepper. Increase heat to medium-high and cook for 7 to 8 minutes. Remove from heat and set aside to cool. Once cooled, add the shredded cheese and grated cheese and mix well.

Sprinkle a clean surface with flour, and stretch out the dough to an oblong shape using a rolling pin. Spread spinach mixture evenly over the dough, leaving a ½-inch border. Roll up the dough lengthwise, jelly-roll style, and pinch the ends closed. Then brush the outside of the dough with the egg white. Place onto prepared cookie sheet and bake for 40 to 45 minutes, until bread is golden brown.

MAKES 10 TO 12 (1½- TO 2-INCH) SLICES

CAESAR SALAD

There is a very delicious restaurant on Staten Island called the Marina Café. It was one of the first to make the Caesar salad in front of you at the table. This is where Jennifer learned how to make it, and spent countless days preparing this for all of us. There was a time that we were so sick of Caesar Salad that we banned her from making it. She got so mad one time while making it for us at the table that she started throwing the eggs at us. Needless to say, we made sure to eat the salad that night for dinner or else she would have thrown another fit. After that, she gave us a little break from the salad but to this day, it still remains one of our favorites. Make sure you try it 'cause you don't want to feel her wrath like we did! You can add chicken, steak, or shrimp to this to make it more of a meal.

1 head romaine lettuce

4 cloves garlic

2–3 anchovies

1⅓ cups extra virgin olive oil

1–2 tablespoons Dijon mustard

½ teaspoon Worcestershire sauce

2 egg yolks

3 tablespoons fresh lemon juice

Salt and pepper, to taste

Freshly grated Parmigiano-Reggiano cheese

1 cup croutons

Freshly shaved Parmigiano-Reggiano cheese

Clean and cut romaine lettuce into 1- or 2-inch pieces, and air-dry or pat dry with paper towels. Place in a large bowl, and set aside.

In a large wooden salad bowl, mash together garlic and anchovies using two forks (tearing the anchovies into small pieces and crushing them together with the garlic). Pour in the olive oil and mix to combine with the anchovy mixture. Add in Dijon mustard and mix together until emulsified. Add in Worcestershire sauce and combine well.

Add the yolks to the mixture and whisk together. Squeeze in the lemon juice and add salt and pepper to taste. Add in the romaine lettuce and toss the salad together with the dressing until the lettuce is fully coated. Sprinkle the grated cheese on top and continue to toss the salad. Garnish with croutons and thin slices of shaved Parmigiano-Reggiano. For a little added zest, squeeze some additional lemon juice on top.

SERVES 4

CAPONATA

Eggplant is the main ingredient in this treat, which Renee can make a whole meal out of. No one loves eggplant as much as Renee, and she can finish the entire dish before everyone gets a chance to try it. This is a family favorite that all of us enjoy. We always have a few eggplants growing in Mom's gardens just in case we have to make this for some guests.

2 large eggplants, cubed

Salt and pepper, to taste

¼ cup olive oil

1 large onion, chopped

2 cups crushed San Marzano tomatoes or fresh plum tomatoes

6 fresh basil leaves, chopped

½ cup green Italian olives, sliced

3 tablespoons salted capers, rinsed

2 stalks celery, diced

4 tablespoons red wine vinegar

2 tablespoons sugar

Place the cubed eggplant in a colander and salt liberally. Place a heavy plate on top of cubes for about 1 hour. Do not rinse the eggplant. In a large frying pan, heat olive oil over medium heat and sauté onion for about 5 minutes. Add the eggplant cubes, turning to brown on all sides, 5 to 6 minutes. Add the crushed tomatoes and basil, and simmer for about 15 minutes. Add the olives, capers, celery, vinegar, and sugar, and simmer for an additional 15 minutes. Serve warm or at room temperature, on toasted Italian bread if you like.

SERVES 6 TO 8

LENTIL SOUP

A classic family recipe that, in truth, is older than all of the sisters combined. Grandma Nora brought this recipe from the old country, and swears it is full of iron. We make this for the kids on cold winter days to warm up their chilly bones after playing in the snow. The fragrant aroma alone could feed the soul.

3 tablespoons olive oil

6 cloves garlic, chopped

1 medium onion, chopped

2 ham steaks, diced (about ½ pound)

4 carrots, peeled and chopped

1 pound lentils (about 1¼ cups)

8 cups chicken stock

Salt and pepper, to taste

1 pound small elbow pasta

¼ cup grated Pecorino-Romano cheese

In a large saucepan, heat the olive oil over medium heat. Add garlic and onion, and sauté until slightly brown, then add the ham. Cook for 3 to 4 minutes. Add carrots, lentils, chicken stock, salt, and pepper. Bring to a boil over high heat. Cover, and simmer over low heat until the lentils are almost tender, 45 to 50 minutes. Fill a large pot with water, bring to a boil, and cook pasta according to package instructions. Ladle the soup into bowls and add whatever amount of pasta you would like to each. Sprinkle each bowl with grated cheese.

SERVES 6 TO 8

ITALIAN WEDDING SOUP

The term "wedding soup" is a mistranslation of the Italian phrase minestra maritata *("married soup"), which is a reference to the fact that green vegetables and meats go well together. Whatever it means, all we can say is that it figures they would include something with little Italian "meatballs" on your wedding night. What a way to start off the honeymoon!*

1 pound tortellini

½ pound ground beef

½ pound ground pork

¾ cup grated Pecorino-Romano cheese, divided

5–6 cloves garlic, chopped, divided

2 tablespoons fresh parsley

1 egg

½ cup seasoned bread crumbs

3 tablespoons olive oil

1 pound fresh baby spinach

Salt and pepper, to taste

8 cups chicken stock

Bring a large pot of water to boil. Cook the tortellini according to package instructions, drain, and set aside.

In a large bowl, combine meats with half of the cheese, half of the garlic, parsley, egg, and bread crumbs. Roll into bite-size balls.

In a 3-quart pot, add the olive oil and heat on medium until oil starts to bubble, then add meatballs. Toss them around, browning them as best as you can. Add remaining garlic and cook for 1 to 2 minutes. Reduce heat to medium-low and add spinach, salt, and pepper, and toss to mix. Slowly add the chicken stock, and cook for 15 to 20 minutes.

Ladle the soup into bowls, add some tortellini, and serve. Top with remaining grated cheese.

SERVES 4 TO 6

ACKNOWLEDGMENTS

I WOULD FIRST LIKE TO THANK the man who has made my life and all my dreams possible: God. Even at the hardest and weakest moments, you've stood by me and rebuilt me as opposed to leaving. I will forever be your servant #childofgod. Second, my parents, you gave me life and love and even more love than I've deserved at times. Like God, you never turned away from me. Third, my son, you are my lifeline, my love, my confidant, and my heir! I love you, buddy. Grandma Nora, you will forever be in my heart and soul. For my sister Lana: I'm happy we are finally in a good place—I love you, Anthony, John, and Sonni! And last but not least, my sister Jennifer—looks like YOU MADE IT!! I can't tell you how proud I am of you and how honored I am not just to be your sister but to work for such a brilliant, strong woman. You have the patience of a saint like Mommy; a business mind like Daddy; and love for your sisters, like your sisters have for you!!!! I think you're a great mother because my nephew, Justin, is a fine young man. Thanks for giving us this opportunity to share our family's recipes with all of our fans. Like I say #GRAZIANOGIRLZGETITDONE.

—*Renee*

I have never professed to be the world's greatest cook, but when I do it, I do it great! As a hectic career woman, cooking is not always the first thing on my list, but my son, Justin, has been my inspiration to learn more and cook more since the day he was born. He has such a love of food and has had a mature palate from day one!! He is the love of my life and I would do anything for him . . . even cook!!! In my effort to please him, I have learned so many recipes from so many different people in my life, and I would like to recognize and thank all the wonderful cooks that have taught me throughout the years: Grandma Nora, who has been my cooking inspiration since childhood. We miss you and wish you were still here to see all of our success. Mom, I have learned all the staples in life from you—chicken cutlets, meat loaf, steak, potatoes, and definitely all my various vegetable frittatas. Dad, you are the seafood king. I remember catching and eating everything with you. I'd also like to thank Jimmy Crinion, my godmother Angie India, and Marilyn for the best veal cutlets (and the only thing she knows how to make—haha). All of you are amazing cooks. My brother-in-law, John—you have also taught me a thing or two in the kitchen; thank you for the best ricotta and eggs on this planet. Thanks to Ramone Cross, who has taught me to add some spice and flavor to my cooking!! Thanks for the best spicy crab sauce recipe in town, as well as all the simple things you taught me to make my dishes even better. To my special sister Renee, I always knew you were a superstar—in and out of the kitchen! When I am in a cooking bind and I really want to impress people I have my "go to" girls—Aunt Celia, Big Ang, and Lana. Thanks to Aunt Celia for my artichokes, shrimp oreganata, and stuffed lobster—now you know why I always call you and ask if you are cooking! To Big Ang, who cracks me up the entire time she is telling me her amazing and delectable recipes, you truly are an amazing person and cook. Last but not least, my sister Lana who makes cooking for thirty to forty people look like a breeze. You are the best modern-day cook I know, and I appreciate everything I am able to learn from you.

—Jennifer

To my grandmother Nora, who was always such an inspiration to me in the kitchen and the best cook I will ever know. Thank you for teaching me how to cook. I love and miss you . . . still. I strive to be like you and hope that one day my children and grandchildren look up to me as much as we all did to you. To my parents, Anthony and Veronica, thank you for all of your love and support. A million thanks to my sister Jennifer, who has given me the opportunity to bring our family's recipes to other families' tables, where I get the chance to make everyone happy through food. Thanks to Renee for not only being a star on television but for being a star in the kitchen with a new flair and an openness for different flavors that I would never have thought of. I also want to thank my late mother-in-law, Rosie, for some of her recipes as well.

—Lana

Lana's mother-in-law, Rosie

INDEX

Page numbers in *italics* represent photographs.

Flank Steak (Grilled) with Arugula, White Beans, Red Onion, and Grape Tomato Salad, 53
Fontina Cheese, Chicken Rolls with, 77
Fried Eggplant, Penne with, *42*, 43
Frittata, Zucchini, 143, 148, *149*
Frutti di Mare, 1, *12*, 13

G

garlic
    Broccoli Rabe with Garlic and Oil, 130, *131*
    Garlic Crabs, 1, 7
    Garlic Shrimp, 8
    Graziano family and, 127
    Italian Cheesy Garlic Bread, 143, 145
    Roasted Leg of Lamb with Rosemary and Garlic, 85, 87
    Zucchini with Garlic and Oil, 115, *126*, 127, 148
    Zuppa Clams in Garlic and Oil, *4*, 5
Gebbia, Anthony (Veronica's father), 58
Gebbia, Nora Eda Amelia Cultura DiMarini (Grandma), *v*, ix, x, 10, 15, 28, 37, 44, 67, 83, 92, 108, 111, 127, 165
goat cheese
    Chicken Cutlet Milanese with Goat Cheese Salad, 65, *82*, 83
    Roasted Beets with Apples and Goat Cheese, 124, *125*
Grape Tomato Salad, Grilled Flank Steak with Arugula, White Beans, Red Onion, and, 53
Gravy, Sunday, 23, 45
Graziano family, ix–xii
    aggression and meatballs, 139
    Alexis, 147
    Anthony (Dad), *v*, x, xi, *xiv*, 1, 5, 10, 13, *22*, 25, 45, *46*, 56, 61, 75, 89, 95, 101, 112, 113, 133, 147, 157
    baccala, 14
    balls and, 141
    basil leaves, 28
    boating memories, *xiv*, 5
    boxing, 56
    Celia (Aunt), 10, *46*
    cheese loved by, 77
    Christmas, 6
    commercializing Italian foods, 67
    crabbing at the Jersey Shore, *xiv*, 7
    dining al fresco, 16
    Easter Sunday, 62, 87
    Gabrielle, 147
    garlic and oil and, 127
    Italian foods, commercializing, 67

Italian soul food, 26
Jamie, 147
Mama Rosa's (Anthony's and Lana's restaurant), xi
Marilyn (Aunt), 52, 147
Minnesota and, 61
New Year's Eve, 13
Nora (Grandma), *v*, ix, x, 10, 15, 28, 37, 44, 67, 83, 92, 108, 111, 127, 165
parties and, 39
prunes and, 111
roast hidden in prison uniform, 61
San Gennaro Feast in Little Italy, 75, 103, 112
sausage and, 112
side jobs and, 115
specialties and, 143
St. Joseph's day, 40
Sundays and, 45
Supreme Macaroni Company in Hell's Kitchen and, x–xi
Veronica (Mom), *v*, x, 1, 5, 10, 16, 21, *22*, 27, 45, *46*, 58, 61, 62, *64*, 78, 80, 83, *84*, 92, 95, 147, 148, 161
Villa Verona on Staten Island (first family restaurant), xi
wine loved by, 68
Wing and a Clam (Anthony's restaurant), xi, 1, 25, 56
See also beef; Italian specialties; Mob family's secrets and recipes; pasta; pork; poultry; sauces; seafood; sides; soups; veal and lamb
Graziano, Jennifer, ix–xii
    Caesar Salad and, 162
    chicken cutlets and, 83
    Justin (Jennifer's son), 57, *84*, 92, 97, 147, 148
    liver (human) and, 52
    Mob Wives (TV show) and, ix, 45
    photos of, *v*, *x*, *xi*, *xiv*, *10*, *22*, *46*, *64*, *84*, *102*, *151*
    recipes, xi, 10, 45, 49, 57, 60, 62, 71, 80, 83, 88, 89, 92, 94, 97, 117, 119, 147, 148, 150, 158, 162
    Supreme Macaroni in Hell's Kitchen and, xi
    zucchini as toy, 44
Graziano, Lana, ix–xii
    aggression and stuffing meats, 49
    Anthony (Lana's son), 43, *64*, *142*, 145, 147
    cooking skills of, x, xi
    John (Lana's ex-husband), 137, 147
    John (Lana's son), *64*, 98, 147
    Lana's Chicken Soup, 70
    Lana's Famous Grilled Corn on the Cob, 53, 137
    Lana's Famous Salad, 111, *118*, 119
    Lana's Meatballs, 45, *138*, 139
    Mama Rosa's (Anthony's and Lana's restaurant), xi

We are excited to announce our very own food and wine brands coming soon, Graziano Macaroni Company and Grazie by Graziano Wines. All of the delicious recipes found in this book can be made with our food and wines, which will be available on GrazianoMacaroni.com and GrazieWines.com and in retail locations across the country.